FUTURE
WORLD ORDER

a global legitimacy crisis ...

... cured by tech?

DR MAHA HOSAIN AZIZ

FUTURE WORLD ORDER

A Global Legitimacy Crisis…

Cured By Tech?

By Dr Maha Hosain Aziz
www.futureworldorder.org

Cover by comic book artist and illustrator Karen Rubins
www.karenrubins.com

Copyright for FUTURE WORLD ORDER © 2019 Maha Aziz

ISBN: 9781091096196

DEDICATION

For my sweet big brother **ABID AZIZ**
(Nov 30, 1974 - Dec 3, 2017),
who always encouraged my creativity

15% of my book profits will be going to the *Abid Aziz Fund*
which supports charity Peace & Sport's Syrian refugee
youth project in Jordan's Za'atari camp

More details at:
https://www.peace-sport.org/in-memory-of-abid-aziz/

EARLY REVIEWS OF
FUTURE WORLD ORDER

DR NOURIEL ROUBINI, Professor of Economics and
International Business at NYU Stern and
CEO of Roubini Macro Associates:
**Dr Aziz has vision. *Future World Order* is the essential guide for
every citizen to understand the major global risks we face –
and consider how we may tackle them. With few female
political thinkers today, Dr Aziz is a welcome addition.
She is definitely a global thinker to watch.**

DR MARGARET LEVI, 2019 Winner of Johan Skytte Prize in Political
Science, Professor of Political Science and Director at Center for
Advanced Study in the Behavioral Sciences at Stanford University
**Highly accessible and thoughtfully argued, *Future World
Order* offers both analysis and blueprint. Aziz is tough-minded
in her reading of the sources of political, economic and social
crisis in our contemporary era. But she also offers a pathway
through the morass. She proposes a new social contract that
can be built from what is promising in technology. *Future
World Order* is sophisticated and stimulating,
its ideas worth taking seriously.**

DR IAN BREMMER, Eurasia Group Founder
& Author of *US vs Them* (2018):
**A book that looks past the headlines to the underlying issues
fueling our current world disorder… then offers some
persuasive optimism that all is not yet lost. When it comes to
political risk, it's hard not to lose sight of the forest for the
trees; this is not a problem for Aziz,
making her book a must-read.**

KISHORE MAHBUBANI, Founding Dean of Lee Kuan Yew School of
Public Policy & Author of *Has the West Lost It?* (2018):
One fact cannot be denied. Global anxiety has gripped even

our young generations on many fronts: geopolitically, politically, economically and socially. Aziz captures and distills the anxiety and thoughtfully suggests how we can leverage the possibilities of technology to get out of it. A must-read.

DANIELLE KAYEMBE, Female Futurist, Author of *The Silent Rise of the Female-Driven Economy* (2017) and CEO of Greyfire Impact:
A rising voice in governance and public policy, Dr Aziz delivers an engaging and thought-provoking read on the future of our increasingly interconnected world. In *Future World Order*, she weaves together the disruptions, transitions and risks created by the global legitimacy crisis and a population learning to leverage technology. In a trust-less world where data is the new currency, *Future World Order* leaves the reader hopeful – Dr Aziz hints at the possibility of a rising, decentralized world on the horizon, powered by informed citizens, technologies like blockchain and shaped by a more inclusive social landscape.

DR PARAG KHANNA, Managing Partner of FutureMap and Author of *Connectography* and *The Future Is Asian* (2019):
It takes an engaged scholar activist like Dr Maha Hosain Aziz to adequately capture the worrying scope of today's overlapping crises of legitimacy. But with her finger on the pulse of the next generation, she also highlights how technology can positively spur citizen engagement to bring about a new social contract – both at the national and global levels.

DOUGLAS RUSHKOFF, Author of *Team Human* (2019):
The systems of government we've been living with are coming down. It's not a matter of if or even when, but how. Aziz shows that accepting and fostering this change is the surest path toward a soft landing, peaceful transition, and sustainable outcome.

More reviews at www.futureworldorder.org

ACKNOWLEDGMENTS

This book is *long* overdue. What can I say – my apologies for the huge delay. Before I get to it, I must first acknowledge those who have influenced my work in distinct ways in recent years:

*my colleagues and grad students in political risk at NYU (MA International Relations Program, Grad School of Arts & Sciences)

*my e-learning students in political risk at Pioneer Academics

*my colleagues in various consulting projects over the years

*long-time mentors Dr Ian Bremmer, Dr Parag Khanna, Dr Asma Siddiki and Michele Wucker who have led by example

*my PhD advisors Dr John Sidel and Dr Matt Nelson who introduced me to the idea of *legitimacy* many years ago

*my column and blog readers over the years, from *Bloomberg Businessweek* to the *Huffington Post* and now *Medium.com*

*last but not least, my close friends worldwide and all members of my global family, Team Aziz-Khan (especially my sweet mother; plus my two nieces and nephew, aged 10 to 20, who hopefully read their favorite (!) aunt's book as they navigate their own futures)

CONTENTS

FUTURE
WORLD ORDER

a global legitimacy crisis ...

... cured by tech?

DR MAHA HOSAIN AZIZ

CHAPTER 1

INTRODUCING OUR GLOBAL LEGITIMACY CRISIS

WELCOME TO MY BOOK

Hello Reader,

How are you? I'm so happy to finally have this opportunity to share my ideas with you. Since 2012, I have devoted my time and energy to making better sense of the world – as a social scientist, frankly I see this as my responsibility. Now, at this sensitive *global* turning point, I feel more committed than ever to share my perspective with more of you so you can make better sense of the world too. We must all be on the same page about what we are facing and how we might tackle it. How can we secure the optimal, or at least a *better*, future world order?

In recent years, through my work as a social scientist, I started to notice some worrisome trends in certain countries, particularly a growing anti-government strain. I also noted that this particular anti-government strain appeared to be evolving into a broader challenge to the status quo in most countries, regardless of political system, level of economic development or social structure. East or West, rich or poor, democratic or nondemocratic, few countries were being spared from this challenge to the status quo – and the truth is it has only gotten worse.

Today, we really are *all* in the same boat with similar threats to our stability. This is what I term a *global legitimacy crisis* that impacts our geopolitics, politics, economics and society. What is a legitimacy crisis, you ask? Effectively, it's a *loss of faith* in a longstanding policy, leader or even an entire system – that leads to some kind of *challenge to the existing status quo*. But more on that in a little bit.

At this point, I should let you know that I do view the world through a very specific and, yes, rather negative lens, of *risk*. Effectively, risk tells you what is going wrong in a particular country, region or the world. But this lens also gives you insight into how things might evolve in the future – it led me to the global legitimacy crisis we face today. I have honed this qualitative analytical approach through my years as a professor focused on political risk & prediction at my home base in the MA International Relations Program at NYU and through past consulting projects on this topic for governments and corporates via Wikistrat[1] and other networks.

In recent years, I began presenting this global legitimacy crisis to specialist audiences so they could be more enlightened about their future – from other professors at academic conferences and researchers and journalists at think tank events to investors and government folk in my consulting work. I have also recurrently shared my ideas with a broader audience through my blogs for *CNN*, the *Observer*, the *Huffington Post* and *Medium.com*. I even drew a political comic book about it (*The Global Kid*[2]) so tweens and teens could be aware about our major global challenges too.

---

[1] Wikistrat is the world's first crowdsourced consultancy which leverages a global crowd of experts in an online platform to analyze complex issues in real-time and make predictions.

[2] *The Global Kid* (2016) is my award-winning political comic book that teaches youth about the global risks we face and how tech might help. All sales went to youth education nonprofits. More details are at: www.theglobalkid.org.

The feedback I have often received is one of disbelief and even anger. Few want to hear the world might be in such terrible shape. This is what some psychologists term cognitive dissonance[3] – that feeling of mental discomfort we experience if one's existing views are challenged by conflicting new information (especially negative information). There seemed to be a notable reluctance to recognize that what was happening in one country in one region of the world was actually happening pretty much everywhere else – that this period of domestic struggle was in fact part of a broader global challenge with no immediate solutions and no identifiable cause.

Many have declared that the major turning point that has unleashed so much of what we are witnessing today was a singular event – US President Donald Trump's victory in the 2016[4] election[5] or the UK's Brexit referendum earlier that year. But that's

[3] Leon Festinger, *Theory of Cognitive Dissonance*, Stanford University Press, 1957

[4] James Kirchick, Blaming Trump For Their Problems Is The One Thing Europeans Can Agree On, *Brookings Institution,* Feb 15, 2019

[5] Graeme Wearden, 'President Trump' As Big a Threat As Jihadi Terror to Global Economy - EIU, *Guardian*, Mar 17, 2016

not the whole picture (even if yes, these events have made, and continue to make, matters worse). The reality is today's negative trends have been building globally since at least 2009 and there is no one singular explanation, one person, or one event to blame for it. This was a long time coming with many factors.

I want to use this one on one time with you, Reader, to explain these deeply rooted trends challenging the status quo and perhaps help you manage your expectations of the world for the coming years. How will our global legitimacy crisis evolve till we get to that elusive *turning point*? Above all, this book aims to be a guide for anyone – from the silent generation to the post-millennial – to better understand the world today and what might come next. It's even more important that we all understand that we *each* have a role to play in achieving a more secure future world order. This is a sensitive global turning point in our existence.

So first, don't panic as I explain how the world is struggling in four key ways – geopolitically, politically, economically and socially – and how tech has already made this struggle worse.

Second, as you read my book, do remind yourselves of the silver lining – that this global legitimacy crisis is also an *opportunity*. This is the crucial time for us to truly reimagine our future with *new* ideas. Don't be shy – be part of the debate, even if you don't agree with my vision here. The cliché in this case is very true: every voice really can make a difference.

UNDERSTANDING GLOBAL RISK & PREDICTION

In his 1555 book of 942 poetic quatrains, *Les Propheties*[6], French visionary Nostradamus[7] apparently predicted everything from the rise of Adolf Hitler to the Great Fire of London to the September 11 terrorist attacks. He also hinted that 2018 would mark the start of a 27-year world war between two major powers. Could that be between the US and China? It does feel that way at times but let's see how that superpower dynamic develops.

---

[6] Michel de Nostredame, *Les Propheties*, Macé Bonhomme, 1555

[7] Áine Cain, Nine Famous Predictions By Nostradamus Some People Say Foresaw the Future, *Business Insider*, May 14, 2018

For those of us without such mysterious predictive powers, we have to rely on qualitative data and analysis to make valued judgements about the future. In this book, my vision for the world implicitly applies a four-tiered risk[8] framework to determine the current threats to stability and consider how these threats might evolve. It boils down to understanding what makes a country tick in terms of its geopolitics, politics, economics and society.

We qualitative researchers painstakingly sift through open source information online, everything from statements from governments and non-state actors, to local and global media, academic theory, think tank reports and political risk research. This allows us to identify risks that might impact geopolitical, political, economic or social stability in a country. Some risks may be glaringly obvious (i.e. gray rhinos)[9] which we should in theory be

---

[8] The quintessential book to read on political risk is *The Fat Tail: The Power of Political Knowledge in an Uncertain World* (Oxford University Press, 2009) by Dr Ian Bremmer, the father of contemporary political risk, and Dr Preston Keat.

[9] Michele Wucker, *The Gray Rhino*, St Martins Press, 2016

able to prepare for, while others are unpredictable shock events (i.e. black swans[10]).

The question we then must answer is whether ruling governments can adequately cope with these obvious and unexpected threats to stability. We evaluate which of these threats might actually lead to a notable change in the status quo. We make our subjective judgments on the most plausible future based on the data at hand. That's all it is really. Applying this risk framework to countries globally, I found that these threats to stability did not discriminate; whatever the political, economic or social makeup of the country, the same threats seemed to be coming up everywhere in the world. These comparable *domestic* threats together represented a *global* risk which kept growing – and this global legitimacy crisis persists today.

Yes, there are other more quantitative approaches to risk that might lead to more precise predictions. For instance, some analysts

---

[10] Dr Nassim Taleb, *The Black Swan*, Random House, 2010

leverage game theory[11], statistics[12] and big data[13]. But even these approaches are not 100% accurate as forecasts. Critics argue that most experts making political predictions are rarely held accountable even if they are wrong; some experts simply offer a perspective in line with their own books or theory, even if the reality has changed[14]. This is often true. As one critic[15] jokingly put it, "Human beings who spend their lives studying the state of the world are poorer forecasters than dart-throwing monkeys"[16] (private note to you, Reader: if you can manage to prove this, I will reimburse you for your book purchase – ha!) The reality is "no one can see precisely how human history will unfold."[17]

---

[11] Clive Thompson, Can Game Theory Predict When Iran Will Get the Bomb?, *New York Times*, Aug 12, 2009

[12] Nate Silver, *The Signal and the Noise, Why So Many Predictions Fail – And Some Don't,* Penguin, 2012

[13] Eric Siegel, *Predictive Analytics: The Power to Predict Who Will Click, Buy, Lie or Die*, Wiley, 2016

[14] Daniel W. Drezner, *The Ideas Industry*, Oxford University Press, 2017

[15] Louis Menand, Everybody's An Expert, *New Yorker*, Dec 5, 2005

[16] Philip Tetlock, *Expert Political Judgement: How Good Is It? How Can We Know?*, Princeton University Press, 2005

[17] Condaleeza Rice and Amy B. Zegart, *Political Risk: How Businesses and Organizations Can Anticipate Global Insecurity*, Twelve Books, 2018

Still, we try. And I try my best in this book to explain what is going wrong today. I try to explain how these risks might get worse in the hope that it will help you to prepare for the future, at least a little bit. There *is* value added in examining a range of data from different sources online with an open mind and then making a nuanced judgment on how things might play out. It's a skill that *can* be learned, as Philip Tetlock and Dan Gardner explain in their book *Superforecasting*. It requires us to be humble, open-minded, analytical and adopt a growth mindset, among other characteristics, often making us better than the experts.[18]

Some risk factors are easier to spot than others. The usual suspects persist in different forms from one year to the next which I'm sure you can guess – from various Middle Eastern conflicts and cyber attacks to global economic weakness, terrorism and

---

[18] Philip Tetlock and Dan Gardner's book, *Superforecasting: The Art and Science of Prediction* (Crown Pubishers, 2016) based their findings for the best forecasters on the Good Judgment Project (GJP); it showed the top GJP forecasters were "30% better than intelligence officers with access to actual classified information" (Alix Spiegel, So You Think You're Smarter than a CIA Agent, *NPR*, Apr 2, 2014).

climate change[19]. These are factors that pose a chronic threat to our stability—that's global risk in a nutshell.

This year, various analysts have highlighted the US-China dynamic, European populism, the US itself[20], water crises[21], different forms of extremism, internet wars[22] and the trade tensions[23] as sources of instability for the world. But other factors, like our global legitimacy crisis, may be less obvious to you even though frankly they feed into all other risks. They are slowly deepening over time such that some governments may ignore them to focus on more immediate risks. It would be an understatement to say this approach is dangerous for our future world order.

A MAJOR GLOBAL RISK:
OUR GLOBAL LEGITIMACY CRISIS

[19] David Wallis-Wells' *The Uninhabitable Earth: Life After Warming* (Tim Duggan Books, 2019) is the book to read if you are curious about how bad global warming will get rather quickly.

[20] Top Risks 2019, Eurasia Group, Jan 7, 2019

[21] Global Risks Report 2019, World Economic Forum, Jan 15, 2019

[22] Maha Hosain Aziz, What Are the Global Risks to Watch in 2019?, *Medium*, Jan 9, 2019

[23] World Economic Outlook Update, IMF, Jan 2019

AND THE TECH FACTOR

In the next four chapters, I present our **global legitimacy crisis** which defines our current world order. I predict this will deepen in the coming years in part *because* of tech; and there will be limited consensus on how to resolve all aspects of this crisis. What is the timeframe for this crisis, you might be wondering – when will this crisis magically shift? That's tough to predict. But I argue the tipping point will likely come when more of us, both governments and citizens, recognize this crisis can be cured, at least in part, by embracing tech as a strategic tool. It will come when we reach what AI expert Kai-Fu Lee[24] terms a peaceful "co-existence with AI" and other tech. This could frankly take years or, more likely, decades.

Others like historian Yuval Noah Harari[25] argue the future will be marked by a world run by super humans and techno-elites

---

[24] Kai-Fu Lee, *AI Superpowers: China, Silicon Valley, and the New World Order*, Houghton Mifflin Harcourt, 2018

[25] Yuval Noah Harari, *Homo Deus: A Brief History of Tomorrow*, Harvill Secker, 2016

while the rest of us slowly disappear... My goodness. Just to be clear, Reader, my prediction in this book is for our world today and the next few years or even decades – *before* we reach that happy tipping point of "synergy between AI and the human heart"[26] as described by Lee and way, *way* before Harari's more apocalyptic future where humanity is largely wiped out (which obviously we hope never happens).

In each chapter, first I explain the status quo of recent years – i.e. in terms of geopolitics, politics, economy or society – and how it has been challenged in different ways. This is effectively our global legitimacy crisis. Second, I consider how tech has already made this challenge to the status quo worse. But third, I argue how tech, if strategically leveraged, can actually be part of the cure to our unique global legitimacy crisis in the future.

In Chapter Two, I focus in on our **geopolitical crisis**. It certainly feels as though the post-Cold War era led by the US is over. Speculation began as early as 2008. This represents a crisis of

---

[26] Kai-Fu Lee, How AI Can Co-Exist with Humans, *Medium*, Oct 18, 2018

legitimacy in our international system. Yes, China has global ambition and other superpowers are rising. We *know* that, but who's in charge? We'll be debating the structure of the international system for a few more years. Is it a bipolar world, multipolar system, or something different altogether that defines the world today? We just don't know yet. But tech will likely be the game changer in power relations and potentially the greatest threat to our stability in terms of AI weaponry with no limitations.

In Chapter Three, I talk about our **political crisis** that's been building since the Arab Spring movement surfaced in 2010. The political status quo has been recurrently challenged by growing numbers of citizens in both democratic *and* nondemocratic countries. We used to think democracy was it – the last stop in our political development. Yet the challenges to democracy today suggest otherwise. Tech, especially social media, has empowered the average citizen to be more engaged and activist against government, but it has also created a chronic crisis of political legitimacy making it harder to govern. I suggest tech, particularly crowdsourcing and blockchain, might ease this legitimacy crisis.

In Chapter Four, I explore our **economic crisis** in which the economic status quo of globalization has been recurrently challenged since 1999. Yes, most world leaders and international institutions like the World Bank and IMF still promote free trade and international cooperation – key markers of globalization – as the best way forward. But the challenge from citizens and now populist leaders cannot be ignored. Then throw in the tech factor as the cloud of automation unemployment looms large. Are we prepared? It doesn't feel like it at the moment. I suggest a moral tech economy, a crowdfund for universal basic income (UBI), and some apps to help those who, yes, will lose jobs to robots.

In Chapter Five, I consider our **social crisis** – perhaps our greatest challenge. Different types of identity conflicts are deepening within countries and across borders globally. The rise of anti-minority, xenophobic and Islamophobic sentiment is obviously alarming. It is what I term a *global identity crisis*. The major question we must all ask ourselves is whether we are globalists or nationalists. There seems to be limited clarity on shared global values – if any even still exist. Instead we see a rise in political figures who are openly xenophobic and extremist groups actively spreading their ideology of hate. Where is the counter-narrative[27] to extremism? I highlight what you should already know – social media's sad role in spreading such hate. But I then consider ways tech can in fact increase our empathy for the *other*, including virtual reality and a mass effort to crowdsource new shared global values, especially among youth.

Finally, in Chapter Six, I **conclude** the book by suggesting the next steps in tackling our global legitimacy crisis, while we await true global and national leadership (however long that may take – nobody honestly knows). I consider how this may be the time to embrace certain activist tech billionaires who are already trying to fill a gap left by weak, ineffective governments and

[27] New Zealand Prime Minister Jacinda Ardern called for a global campaign against racism after the March 15 attack on two mosques in Christchurch. This campaign would be a step in the right direction *if* other world leaders participate (John Haltiwanger, New Zealand's Prime Minister Calls For a Global Fight Against Racism and an End to Scapegoating Immigrants After Mass Shooting, *Business Insider*, Mar 20, 2019)

prepare us for a tech economy (and relax – I don't mean Facebook founder Mark Zuckerberg[28], not now anyway[29]). And I consider a more prominent role for the tech-savvy citizen in devising some kind of social contract *with* tech firms. There's a need to recognize the new influencers in our geopolitics, politics, economics and society, including the activist billionaire, the citizen and tech itself.

Many of you may find my perspective on the world today – a global legitimacy crisis worsened by tech – rather bleak. Fair enough. It *is* important for us to take a minute to appreciate the fact that yes, there has been so much progress in so many ways in recent decades. This is exemplified by the ideas of public intellectuals like Steven Pinker and the late Hans Rosling. Pinker[30] explains how factors like health, prosperity, safety, peace, knowledge and happiness are in fact on the rise globally. Rosling[31]

[28] Facebook Faces a Reputational Meltdown, *The Economist*, Mar 22, 2018

[29] Mark Sullivan, On CNN, Mark Zuckerberg Scrambles to Rebuild Trust, *Fast Company*, Nov 21, 2018

[30] Steven Pinker, *Enlightenment Now: The Case for Reason, Science, Humanism and Progress*, Viking, 2018

[31] Hans Rosling, *Factfulness: Ten Reasons We're Wrong About the World – and Why Things Are Better Than We Think*, Flatiron Books, 2018

encourages us to change our pessimistic mindset and be more optimistic about our future – even if things are bad, they are better than they used to be, with less poverty, disease and illiteracy. Yes, point taken. We should celebrate our progress – we *must*.

But that doesn't mean our global legitimacy crisis is not a serious problem, nor should it be swept under the rug. It *is* a rather unique risk we face – the lack of consensus in four major areas of our lives, with our geopolitics, our politics, our economics and our social values. We need some clarity urgently. As humans, we crave it. At its core, this is an ideological battle which creates anxiety and simply can't be measured in quantitive indicators. Nor can it be instantly fixed with one policy or one leader. It really does require our sustained attention *and* all of our participation.

Again, our future world order will be defined by whether we see this global legitimacy crisis as an *opportunity* for more of us to think about what we want. What ideas should shape our geopolitics, politics, economy and society in our world today and in the future? What can we do as empowered, tech-savvy citizens to overcome some of these risks, while our governments muddle through for the foreseeable future?

So, let's get started, Reader. Here's my vision for the world today based on my years as a social scientist who teaches, consults on, blogs about and even draws her speciality of global risk and prediction. Remember these risks have been building for a few years. And it's important to reflect on how it may likely play out. This is our future world order – a global legitimacy crisis worsened by tech. But which we may be able to cure, at least in part, when we fully embrace tech as a strategic tool.

CHAPTER 2

GEOPOLITICAL CRISIS

THE END OF US HEGEMONY

Let's start with an easy pop quiz. Who won the Cold War ending in 1991? Yes – undoubtedly it was the US who beat the former Soviet Union. As you know, the Cold War was a period of tension between the democratic US and communist Soviet Union, and their respective allies spanning four decades. At its core, it was an ideological battle but these two superpowers fought several proxy wars, including Vietnam, Korea, Afghanistan, the Cuban Missile Crisis and the Berlin blockade.

The US thereby earned its hegemonic status in the world, making it *the* superpower of the world – i.e. the "state with the capacity to act globally and the potential to change the whole system."[32] Post-Cold War, the widely held assumption was that no major powers could match the US in four key dimensions of power

---

[32] Christopher Hill, *Changing Politics of Foreign Policy*, Palgrave Macmillan, 2003

– military, economic, technological and cultural – that "cumulatively" gave it "global political clout"[33]. As hegemon, it could "persuade or reward subordinates rather than immediately coercing them"[34]. Its hard and soft power[35] effectively made it "unchallengeable"[36].

In academic theory, we defined this post-Cold War era as unipolar[37] in which the US, as global hegemon, had the political caché to effectively set the global agenda for the rest of us. This agenda promoted liberal democracy and human rights to the international community (whether or not all countries agreed with these values is a separate matter of course). Other states, in theory, had no choice but to exist and compete within the framework established by the hegemon and this system gave stability to the

---

[33] Zbigniew Brzezinski, *The Grand Chessboard: American Primacy and Its Geostrategic Imperatives*, Basic Books, 1997

[34] Elke Krahmann, American Hegemony or Global Governance? Competing Visions of International Security, *International Studies Review*, Vol. 7, No. 4, pg 531-545, Dec 2005

[35] Joseph Nye, *Soft Power: The Means to Success in World Politics*, Public Affairs, 2005

[36] Josef Joffe, How America Does It, *Foreign Affairs*, Sept/Oct 1997

[37] Michael Mastanduno & Ethan Kapstein, *Unipolar Politics: Realism and State Strategies After the Cold War*, Columbia University Press, 1999

world. US presidents, from Bill Clinton to Barack Obama recurrently reminded us that the US was "indispensable" in international affairs.

But a lot has changed. Could America's unipolar moment[38] be over[39]? It does feel that way. Yes, we all know about President Trump's unilateral, "America First"[40] rhetoric. The international system appears to be headed away from a unipolar system, after years of US leadership post-Cold War. The geopolitical status quo has been challenged. We are witnessing a major crisis of legitimacy in our international system.

But the truth is academics, analysts, journalists and policymakers have been debating the decline[41] of US hegemony[42]

---

[38] Charles Krauthmatter, The Unipolar Moment, *Foreign Affairs*, America and the World 1990 Issue

[39] Ian Bremmer, The Era of American Leadership Is Over, *Time*, Dec 19, 2016

[40] Howard Stoffer, What Trump's 'America First' Policy Could Mean for the World, *Time*, Nov 14, 2016

[41] Parag Khanna, Waving Goodbye to US Hegemony, *New York Times Magazine*, Jan 2, 2008

[42] Noam Chomsky, America Is An Empire In Decline, *Salon*, May 10, 2016

recurrently since the end of the Cold War[43]. What was the turning point? Well, I remember when I was in college back at Brown University, the Sept 11 attacks happened – and for the first time, as budding IR scholars, my peers and I started to question our professors as to whether the US *was* in fact vulnerable, especially to external security threats. Could it really be the leading hegemon after such an overt challenge?

Years later, while I was at grad school at the London School of Economics, the 2008 global economic crisis occurred – again we started to question whether US economic power was *as* susceptible to weakness as any other country, perhaps even more so with its subprime mortgage crisis triggering the Great Recession. With threats to its security and its economy, could the US *still* be labelled the leading hegemonic power? Fast forward to 2017 to President Trump's anti-globalist rhetoric which confirms, at least for now, a *different* role for the US in world affairs. However you characterize the turning point, today we are in the

---

[43] Christopher Layne, The Waning of US Hegemony – Myth or Reality? A Review Essay, *International Security*, Vol. 34, No. 1, pg 147-172, Summer, 2009

midst of a major crisis of legitimacy in our international system which itself is a risk – a threat to our stability. It begs the larger question...

WHAT *IS* THE NEW WORLD ORDER?

This is where it gets tricky. It's one thing to say it is *not* a US-led world anymore. But what is it? What is the world in which we now live? This is *not* a post-Cold War era where international alliances are easy to understand and US leadership is clear in its global agenda. Again, President Trump has explicitly and repeatedly said how it's not his job to "represent the world"[44] or impose American "values"[45] (or *his* values?) on other countries. Okay, we get it. But it still feels like a mixed bag at times, perhaps reflecting a *selective hegemony* – when the US government feels like taking a leading role abroad, it does; when it doesn't feel like it, it doesn't. Or is *transactional hegemony* a better way to describe

[44] Remarks by President Trump in Joint Address to Congress, *www.WhiteHouse.Gov*, Feb 28, 2017

[45] Remarks by President Trump to the 72nd Session of the United Nations General Assembly, *www.WhiteHouse.Gov,* Sept 19, 2017

it? (*Or* has that always been the case? Major public intellectuals like Noam Chomsky[46] have made this argument powerfully for many decades.)

Let's consider an example like Syria. Reportedly visibly shaken[47] by photos of children suffering from chemical attacks launched by Syrian President Bashar Assad's government, President Trump initiated airstrikes[48] with France and the UK in 2018. Does this mean on some issues, the US *is* still leading the way in promoting certain global values like human rights? It's hard to say. Consider Venezuela. Different countries are supporting different sides[49] in President Nicolas Maduro's political crisis. The US National Security Advisor John Bolton said it is in the US' interest to oust the autocratic leader to protect Venezuelan

---

[46] The quintessential book to read on the controversial US agenda globally is Chomsky's book *Hegemony or Survival: America's Quest for Global Dominance* (Penguin, 2004).

[47] Michael Shear and Michael Gordon, 63 Hours: From Chemical Attack to Trump's Strike in Syria, *New York Times*, Apr 7, 2017

[48] W. J. Hennigan, Trump Orders Strikes on Syria Over Chemical Weapons, *Time*, Apr 13, 2018

[49] Bianca Britton, 'Pouring Gas On Fire': Russia Slams Trump's Stance in Venezuela, *CNN*, Jan 24, 2019

democracy and human rights. Then again, he also admitted that supporting regime change there was about Venezuela's vast oil reserves[50] and related "business opportunities"[51] for US companies.

Regardless, come 2024 (or 2020?), a new US president may not necessarily guarantee that America's role in the world reverts to what it once was – nor will other major powers or non-state actors worldwide necessarily want that. Frankly, it will be impossible to reseal this ugly can of worms that has been unsealed in geopolitics. But for now, how might we define our international system? The lack of clarity in answering this question is part of our global legitimacy crisis. Let's investigate the possibilities, starting with the most obvious.

The world could be *multipolar*, as many have been speculating for at least a decade. Superpowers Russia, China and the EU have been challenging US hegemony – militarily,

---

[50] Stuart Varney interview with John Bolton, *Fox Business*, Jan 24, 2019

[51] 'Good for Business': Trump Adviser Bolton Admits US interest in Venezuela's 'Oil Capabilities', *RT*, Jan 28, 2019

economically and/or politically – for awhile. Since Trump's presidency began in January 2017, they have stepped up their game.

We all know Russia has been strutting its stuff militarily for years – the 2014 Crimea invasion was no accident; but it is now more openly focused on hybrid warfare[52] in the EU and the US, plus proxy wars in places like the Arctic[53], Afghanistan and Syria. In response to the US pulling out of trade deals like the TPP, China has boldly presented itself as the de-facto leader of globalization since the 2017 World Economic Forum in Davos. In response to President Trump pulling out of the Paris Climate Accords in 2017, the EU – in this case led by France's President Emmanuel Macron – vowed to "Make the Planet Great Again" even inviting American climate scientists to continue their research on French soil.[54]

[52] Reid Standish and Emily Tamkin, Europe and US Move to Fight Russian Hybrid Warfare, *Foreign Policy*, 2017

[53] Paul Watson, A Melting Arctic Could Spark a New Cold War, *Time*, May 12, 2017

[54] Greg Wilford, Emmanuel Macron Offers Refuge to American Climate Scientists After Donald Trump Takes US Out of Paris Climate Deal, *Independent*, June 3, 2017

Collectively, these superpowers are more aggressively shaping the world – because well, they *can*, due to a US superpower with a less consistent global vision.

Then again, maybe the international system today isn't multipolar (or bipolar for that matter, as some would argue with the US and China techonomic cold war[55] brewing). Could this simply be Zakaria's *post-American world*[56]? In his 2008 book of the same name, he acknowledges the US is in decline but the larger issue to note is the rise of other countries, especially economically. As he explains, "the tallest building in the world is now in Dubai, the biggest factory in the world is in China, the largest oil refinery is in India, the largest investment fund in the world is in Abu Dhabi, the largest Ferris wheel in the world is in Singapore." This is all happening while, he contends, the US loses its economic grip in key areas.

---

[55] Unresolved: The Techonomic Cold War with China, Intelligence Squared US Debate, Feb 25, 2019

[56] Fareed Zakaria, *Post-American World*, W. W. Norton, 2008

Or are we still living in Bremmer's *G-Zero[57] world*? In his 2012 book of the same name[58], Bremmer aptly captures the leadership vacuum we have been facing for awhile in geopolitics. Again, keep in mind he foresaw this long before President Trump took office and declared an anti-globalist position. No single country or group of countries has the will or capability, economically or politically to drive the global agenda. Who even has the legitimacy today to *define* the global agenda? This is not a G7, G8 or a G20 world, he argues. This is the era of G-Zero where no one country even wants to take charge.

Others argue that certain non-Western regions are or soon will be dominating the international system. In *Has the West Lost It?[59]*, Kishore Mahbubani makes a strong case for a new world order where the "West" can no longer impose its ideology or military strength on other countries as it simply lacks the

---

[57] Ian Bremmer and Nouriel Roubini, A G-Zero World: The New Economic Club Will Produce Conflict, Not Cooperation, *Foreign Affairs*, Mar/Apr 2011 Issue

[58] Ian Bremmer, *Every Nation for Itself: Winners and Losers in a G-Zero World*, Portfolio, 2012

[59] Kishore Mahbubani, *Has The West Lost It? A Provocation*, Allen Lane, 2018

legitimacy abroad – and it has no coherent strategy. This is in part due to the economic powerhouses of India and China and other Asian players, a story which he feels the Western media is not sufficiently offering us. In the *Future Is Asian*[60], Parag Khanna enlightens us on the particulars of Asia's rise. He astutely points out that Asia is diverse and vast, with five billion people contributing to two-thirds of global economic growth. It's not just about China's rise – it's about *Asia's* rise in a multipolar world *and* multipolarity within Asia itself.

Others argue our world order is going be dominated not by the West or Asia – but by *Africa*. By 2035, the number of young people who are working age in the continent will exceed that of the rest of the world combined – this trend will persist every year till the end of the century. By 2050, one in every four humans will be African. In fact, at the end of the century, nearly 40 percent of the world's population will be African.[61] And here's one

---

[60] Parag Khanna, *Future Is Asian: Commerce, Conflict & Culture in the 21st Century*, Simon & Schuster, 2019

[61] Salih Booker and Ari Rickman, The Future Is African – and the United States Is Not Prepared, *Washington Post*, June 6, 2018

DR MAHA HOSAIN AZIZ

more powerful data point – Africa will account for more than half (54%) of the 2.4 billion global population growth in the coming decades.[62] Are we headed for an international system marked by regional superpowers?

Or forget about regions – maybe our world order will simply see the return of *empires,* as Bernard-Henri Lévy investigates in his new book, *Empire and the Five Kings*[63]. As the US retreats from its post-Cold War role, Lévy argues that these five empires – Russia, China, Turkey, Iran, and Sunni radical Islamism – are taking steps to undermine the liberal values that have been a hallmark of Western civilization.

But wait a minute – maybe thinking about superpowers, specific regions, or empires is not even the full picture. In his book *End of Power*, Moises Naim[64] considers how the nature of power

[62] John McKenna, Six Numbers that Prove the Future Is African, *World Economic Forum*, May 2, 2017

[63] Bernard-Henri Levy, *Empire and the Five Kings: America's Abdication and the Fate of the World*, Henry Holt & Co, 2019

[64] Moises Naim, *The End of Power: From Boardrooms to Battlefields and Churches to States, Why Being In Charge Isn't What It Used To Be*, Basic Books, 2014

has changed today. He suggests that power "shifting from one continent or country to another, or that it is dispersing among many new players, is not enough." What's significant is that the very nature of power is decaying as once dominant "megaplayers" are cut down to size by "microplayers" like inventors, activists and even terrorists who leverage tech and other tools to exert their influence.

On some level, I must admit I agree with the logic of all of these theorists. Of course we will continue to witness the rise of Asia, Africa, certain empires and "microplayers", while superpower multipolarity plays out with different issues and global leadership is still up for grabs. And yes, we'll keep debating where the US fits into his picture – how will it redefine itself long-term? What underlies all of this is that this is a *post-hegemonic world*.[65] And I believe it's a world which derives legitimacy from many key influencers – state *and* non-state – and for now, you know what? Maybe that's ok as we navigate our unique global legitimacy crisis.

---

[65] Maha Hosain Aziz with Doreen Horschig, Yu-Ting (Wendy) Sun, Arsh Harjani and Yueyue Jiang, It's a Post-Hegemonic World and That's OK, *Huffington Post*, July 1, 2017

Yes, superpowers will keep reacting to the US in distinct ways. And collectively, these superpowers will keep aggressively shaping the post-hegemonic world – because well, they can, due to a US with less global vision[66] for the moment. But what we must consider is the less obvious role of smaller states as key influencers in our current world order.

Let's consider an example – human rights. The US government historically has been the global promoter of human rights, but for now there is a shift away from[67] that.[68] In response to President Trump's travel ban[69] and his attempted block on the country's refugee program, Canada has more aggressively welcomed[70] refugees into its borders. As Canadian Prime Minister Justin Trudeau put it in his Tweet back in January 2017: "To those

[66] Chris Strohm, US Intelligence Warns That Russia and China Are Seizing on Global Turmoil, *Bloomberg*, Jan 22, 2019

[67] Imogen Foulkes, Why the UN Is Wary of the US Position on Human Rights, *BBC*, May 9, 2017

[68] Suzanne Nossel, It's OK That Trump Doesn't Care about Human Rights, *Foreign Policy*, June 19, 2017

[69] Matt Taibbi, The Anti-Refugee Movement Is America at Its Most Ignorant, *Rolling Stone,* Feb 1, 2017

[70] Nicolas Kristof, Canada, Leading the Free World, *New York Times*, Feb 4, 2017

fleeing persecution, terror & war, Canadians will welcome you, regardless of your faith. Diversity is our strength."[71]

In response to President Trump's executive order[72] to ban federal money for international groups performing abortions in developing countries, the Netherlands[73] and Norway[74] immediately committed $10 million each in a new fund, with Sweden, Denmark, Luxembourg and others also pledging support. And in response to President Trump's position on climate change, more than 7,400 city mayors[75] globally vowed[76] to fill the US leadership void to tackle this issue – in fact California Governor Jerry Brown[77] sidestepped President Trump to sign an international

---

[71] Rob Gillies, Trudeau Says Canada Will Take Refugees Banned By US, *PBS*, Jan 28, 2017

[72] Netherlands Government to Counter Trump Abortion Funding Ban, *BBC*, Jan 25, 2017

[73] Dutch Commit $10 Million to Replace Lost US Abortion Funding, *Reuters*, Jan 28, 2017

[74] Jon Sharman, Norway Joins Dutch International Abortion Fund to Combat Donald Trump's Aid Ban, *Independent*, Feb 21, 2017

[75] Daniel Boffey, Mayors of 7,400 Cities Vow to Meet Obama's Climate Commitments, *Guardian*, June 28, 2017

[76] Lizette Alvarez, Mayors, Sidestepping Trump, Vow to Fill Void on Climate Change, *New York Times*, June 26, 2017

[77] Reid Wilson, California Signs Deal with China to Combat Climate Change, *The Hill*, June 6, 2017

agreement with China to reduce greenhouse gas emissions. Collectively, these smaller state actors are more aggressively shaping the post-hegemonic world – because again, they can, due to a US with less global vision.

Non-state actors, beyond traditional civil society, are the relatively newer influencers in our post-hegemonic world. Since 2017, we have witnessed the power of the citizen protester to be more globally united, for instance against President Trump's rhetoric on issues like women's rights[78], immigration[79] and climate change[80]. Such activism has of course been facilitated by social media – a reminder of how tech companies are also a key non-state influencer in our post-hegemonic world, perhaps more powerful at times in shaping society than governments. Are these smaller states and non-state actors a permeant feature of our international

---

[78] Ralph Ellis, Protesters Across Globe Rally for Women's Rights, *CNN*, Jan 22, 2017

[79] Chelsea Bailey and Katie Wong, Global Demonstrations Over Trump's Policies Heat Up Amid Anger Over Travel Ban, *NBC News*, Feb 4, 2017

[80] Helen Davidson and Oliver Milman, Global 'March for Science' Protests Call for Action on Climate Change, *Guardian*, Apr 22, 2017

system? And more importantly, could they ease our global legitimacy crisis?

HOW TECH IS INCREASING
GEOPOLITICAL INSTABILITY

Clearly there are many ways to think about today's international system and how it is evolving. We are all offering our best guesses as events unfold with each day. And we each have a right to keep making our judgements about the current world order. Collect your own data, Reader, and give *your* best guess, updating your ideas as new issues arise – this is your right and frankly responsibility in today's evolving world order. But we may also have to consider further how the very *nature* of power is changing and will continue to change in the future. What will this mean for the structure of our international system?

Again, a superpower traditionally is defined by its dominant position globally in terms of its economy, diplomacy, culture and of course military. Yet military strength[81] is also changing – it's no longer just about conventional weapons or even nuclear weapons. Like with many issues today, it boils down to tech.

Tech is already changing the very nature of power, especially military power – and will likely be the game changer for determining the next leading superpower of the international system. The consensus amongst superpowers Russia, US and China seems to be that AI will be key to their national security in the future. In fact, AI could revolutionize military[82] power – and war – as much as nuclear arms has done, according to a 2017 Harvard report[83]. The report explains "why technologies like drones with bird-like agility, robot hackers, and software that generates photo-real fake video are on track to make the American military and its rivals much more powerful."[84]

---

[81] Christopher Woody, These Are the 25 Most Powerful Militaries in the World – and There's a Clear Winner, *Business Insider*, June 18, 2018

[82] Maha Hosain Aziz, #2 Could a Global AI Treaty Be Key to Future Stability?, *Medium*, June 29, 2018

[83] Greg Allen and Taniel Chan, AI and National Security, *Harvard Belfer Center for Science and International Affairs*, 2017

[84] Tom Simonite, AI Could Revolutionize War As Much As Nukes, *Wired*, July 19, 2017

Who will win the new AI weapons race? Russian President Vladimir Putin has openly said that the country with the best AI will "become the ruler"[85] of the world. This may be why his country has already publicly declared it will build "killer robots"[86] no matter what. China has plans to dominate all types of AI by 2030 including weaponry to beat[87] out competition[88] from the current leader– the US.[89] Some argue the US is "already "losing its edge in the global AI research race."[90]

Tech is going to be the game changer in securing power in the international system. AI on the battlefield is the next major

[85] David Meyer, Vladimir Putin Says Whoever Leads in Artificial Intelligence Will Rule the World, Sept 4, 2017

[86] Harold C. Hutchison, Russia Says It Will Ignore Any UN Ban of Killer Robots, Nov 30, 2017

[87] Bill Gertz, AI Weapons: China and America Are Desperate to Dominate This New Technology, National Interest, May 30, 2018

[88] Tom O'Connor, Will Robots Fight the Next War? US and Russia Bring Artificial Intelligence to the Battlefield, Newsweek, Jan 30, 2018

[89] Matt Stroud, The Pentagon Is Getting Serious About AI Weapons: "We must see to it that we cannot be surprised," says the Pentagon's top scientist, Verge, Apr 12, 2018

[90] Jon Christian, Bill Gates Compares Artificial Intelligence to Nuclear Weapons, Futurism, Mar 19, 2018

arms race – in fact it has begun.[91] The question is how do we manage this new type of race so it doesn't lead to the next major conflict or even a world war?

TECH CURES: AN AI WEAPONS TREATY AND A GLOBAL CITIZEN CAMPAIGN

An AI weapons treaty is the next logical step to help secure our future global stability. Thinkers like Anthony Giddens have argued for a magna carta[92] to make sure tech companies don't abuse their power; I've called for some kind of social contract to build a fair relationship between tech companies and the citizen (see Chapter 6). But what about *weaponized* tech? Some regulation of all states (and private companies developing such tech) is absolutely needed for AI on the battlefield.

---

[91] Tom Simonite, For Superpowers, AI Fuels New Global Arms Race, *Wired*, Sept 8, 2017

[92] Anthony Giddens, A Magna Carta for the Digital Age, *Washington Post*, May 2, 2018

Companies like Google[93] have recurrently declared they will *not*[94] allow their AI tech to be used in weapons, at least not since Project Maven (a Pentagon defense contract for image recognition tech that could have been used for drone strikes). That's nice to hear. But then you have the US military itself offering cash prizes of $200,000 to startups[95] that can develop new weapons technology and defense contractors like Lockheed Martin[96] developing such tech for the US Department of Defense, which plans to spend $20 billion[97] on this in 2019 alone. Where is this headed?

In 2017, Elon Musk and 116 other leaders of robotics and AI companies signed a petition to the UN urging it to ban lethal autonomous weapons or more specifically "killer robots" (which

---

[93] Sean Hollister, Google's Project Maven Work Could Have Been Weaponized, Ex-Pentagon Official Admits, *CNET*, June 26, 2018

[94] Paresh Dave, Google Bars Uses of Its Artificial Intelligence Tech in Weapons, *Reuters*, June 7, 2018

[95] Rachel Kraus, The US Army Will Give Startups Who Invent New Weapons a Cash Prize, *Mashable*, June 22, 2018

[96] Amanda Macias, Weapons of the Future: Here's the New War Tech Lockheed Martin Is Pitching to the Pentagon, *CNBC*, March 6, 2018

[97] Jon Harper, Pentagon Set to Boost Spending on High-Tech Armaments, *National Defense*, June 27, 2018

some companies are already developing[98], reportedly in the US, China, Russia and Israel). This year, Human Rights Watch and a group of scientists have renewed the call for a ban on AI weapons at the American Association for the Advancement Science meeting in DC[99], while others, including former US Secretary of State Henry Kissinger, warn AI arms control may never be possible.[100] There has been limited progress with implementing the proposed UN ban since then. Yes, we have more immediate global risks – terrorism, economic crises, climate change and so on. But tech could ultimately be the greatest threat to geopolitical stability, leading to war.

For many years, we have worried about terrorist groups getting access to nuclear weapons – experts[101] already warn of the risk of them gaining access to AI weaponry "in the very near

[98] James Vincent, Elon Musk and AI Leaders Call for a Ban on Killer Robots: 116 experts in the field have signed a petition as UN talks on the subject are delayed, Verge, Aug 21, 2017

[99] Pallab Ghosh, Call to Ban Killer Robots in Wars, BBC, Feb 15, 2019

[100] Will Knight, AI Arms Control May Not Be Possible, Warns Henry Kissinger, MIT Technology Review, Mar 1, 2019

[101] Brian Wheeler, Terrorists 'Certain' to Get Killer Robots, Says Defence Giant, BBC, Nov 30, 2017

future." And some (like Musk) warn AI will spark World War 3. For future stability, why not develop an AI weapons treaty now, alongside other weapons treaties[102] (e.g. nuclear, biological, chemical)?

There's also a role for you to tackle our geopolitical crisis and the potential AI weapon wars, Reader. This is, after all, the era of social media campaigns that are challenging leaders and policies we don't agree with. You could launch your *own* campaign to ban AI weaponry and introduce a treaty to ban it. Or support Musk's petition to the UN. Be informed – get involved.

But big picture, you could also be part of the redesign for our international system. At this year's Munich Conference for the transatlantic security community, the divide between the US and its long-time European allies couldn't have been more obvious. As its organizer and former German ambassador to the US put it, "We have a real problem."[103] But the conference also marked the launch

---

[102] Treaty on the Non-Proliferation of Nuclear Weapons (NPT), United Nations

[103] Marc Champion, 'We Have a Real Problem.' U.S. Is at Odds With European Allies, Munich Meeting Shows, *Time*, Feb 17, 2019

of the *Declaration of Principles*, led by citizens, former government officials, citizens and private entities linked to DC-based think tank Atlantic Council. This document aims to unite the democratic world and remind us of the post-Cold War values of a rule-based international order.

Former US Secretary of State Madeleine Albright explained: "For the past seven decades, free nations have drawn upon the shared values to advance freedom, increase prosperity, and secure peace. But the growing threat from actors who wish to reverse these freedoms, as well as growing skepticism of democracy's value means it's time for citizens around the world who care about these values to stand up and make their voices heard. We need to make clear what we stand for and what kind of world we want to live in."[104]

Former Swedish prime minister Carl Bildt added: "The goal is to reaffirm support for the principles that have been at the foundation of the international order since the end of World War II:

---

[104] David Wemer, Now is the Time to Fight for Freedom, Prosperity, and Peace, Global Democratic Leaders Say, *Atlantic Council Blog*, Feb 24, 2019

democracy; free, fair, and open markets; and the rule of law. We cannot sit idly by while autocrats and demagogues undermine these core principles." This is a remarkable step forward led by former leaders but calls for citizen participation.

More of these global campaigns will come up in the coming years as we muddle through and hope to reorient the world. Get involved to help redefine our international system. Or at the very least, in your homes and larger communities wherever you are in the world, have these important discussions. Be engaged, no matter your age, national background or education. Debate the world order and how things may unfold. What do *you* think?

Is this still a US-led order? If not, what is it – or what would you like it to be, Reader?

CHAPTER 3

POLITICAL CRISIS

DEMOCRACY OR DICTATORSHIP, DOES IT EVEN MATTER ANYMORE?

If you're reading this and you're a politician, there's a chance at some point during your tenure you may very well have been slapped.[105] In fact, in recent years, frustrated citizens have not only slapped their government officials (e.g. in Nepal[106], India[107], Italy[108]), they have thrown food at them (e.g. in Brazil[109], Germany[110], Australia[111], France[112]), set themselves on fire outside

[105] Maha Hosain Aziz, The Age of Protests, *CNN*, April 23, 2012

[106] Joanna Jolly, Nepal: Man Who Hit Politician Hailed 'A Hero', *BBC*, Jan 26, 2011

[107] India Agriculture Minister Sharad Pawar Slapped, *BBC*, Nov 24, 2011

[108] Telegraph Video, Protester Slaps Italian Far-Right Politician, *Telegraph*, Nov 9, 2014

[109] Maya Oppenheim, Brazilian Politician Pelted with Eggs By Protesters at Her Own Wedding, *Independent*, July 16, 2017

[110] Telegraph Video, German MP Slapped in the Face with Chocolate Cake Over Stance on Refugees, May 29, 2016

[111] Megan McCluskey, Teen in Viral Video Eggs Australian Politician Who Blamed Immigration for New Zealand Mosque Shootings, *Time*, Mar 16, 2019

[112] Nicholas Vinocur, Emmanuel Macron Pelted with Eggs by Angry Mob, *Politico*, Mar 6, 2016

state offices (e.g. in Morocco[113], Greece[114]), launched mass demonstrations to protest specific policies (e.g. in Chile[115], Portugal[116]) and, for better or worse, even brought down entire regimes (e.g. MENA).

There's no doubt about it – it's a tough time to be a politician anywhere in the world. Democracy or dictatorship, citizens are recurrently, and in some cases chronically, unhappy with their governments – and they are not afraid to show it. This is what I term a *crisis of political legitimacy*[117] where the political status quo is being aggressively challenged by citizens; it is one part of our larger global legitimacy crisis. But why is this happening and what does this all mean for our broader political development?

---

[113] Lilia Blaise, Self-Immolation, Catalyst of the Arab Spring, Is Now a Grim Trend, *New York Times*, July 9, 2017

[114] Teo Kermeliotis, Austerity Drives Up Suicide Rate in Debt-Ridden Greece, *CNN*, Apr 6, 2012

[115] Clashes in Chile as Thousands of Students Protest Lagging Education Reform, *RT*, Aug 22, 2014

[116] Thousands Rally Against Portuguese Austerity, *Al Jazeera*, Oct 19, 2013

[117] Maha Hosain Aziz, Why Trump's Win Isn't So Shocking: A Six Year Glbal Crisis of Political Legitimacy, *Huffington Post*, Nov 28. 2016

What we've been witnessing is the decline of state-society relations in which increasing numbers of citizens no longer believe in their leaders, governments, political systems or certain policies – and they are speaking out in violent and non-violent ways. There's a recurring feeling that there *must* be a better, more legitimate way to govern, even if the alternative is not always apparent.

The truth is citizens have been notably unhappy in both democratic and nondemocratic countries for many years. In fact, certain polls[118] and especially groundbreaking studies[119] like that of Yascha Mounk and Roberto Stefan Foa reveal[120] citizens, especially millennials, in long-standing democracies don't really care as much about democracy[121] anymore. This is a significant shift to say the least. Even theorist Francis Fukuyama who once declared democracy was the final stage in our political

---

[118] Michael Safi, Have Millennials Given Up On Democracy?, *Guardian*, Mar 18, 2016

[119] Rebecca Burgess, Have Millennials Fallen Out of Love with Democracy? *Newsweek*, Sept 2, 2016

[120] Yascha Mounk and Roberto Stefan Foa, Yes, People Really Are Turning Away From Democracy, *Washington Post*, Dec 8, 2016

[121] Yascha Mounk, *People vs Democracy: Why Our Freedom Is In Danger and How to Save It,* Harvard University Press, 2018

development – or the "end of history"[122], as he put it back in 1989 – now fears[123] for its future. And of course let's not forget it's a post-hegemonic world where, for now anyway, democracy[124] promotion[125] is no longer a major foreign policy objective of the US government.

Let's consider a few (but of course, not all) empirical examples of challenges to the political status quo over the years. Perhaps the first example of the frustrated citizen was the self-immolating fruit seller[126] in Tunisia fed up with government corruption back in 2010, which sparked revolutionary protests against dictators in many countries in the MENA region; yes, it

---

[122] Francis Fukuyama, End of History, *National Interest*, No. 16, pg 3-18, Summer 1989

[123] Ishaan Tharoor, The Man Who Declared the "End of History" Now Fears for Democracy's Future, *Washington Post*, Feb, 9, 2017

[124] Josh Rogin, State Department Considers Scrubbing Democracy Promotion from Its Mission, *Washington Post*, Aug 1, 2017

[125] Jennifer Rubin, Why Editing Out Democracy Matters, *Washington Post*, Aug 1, 2017

[126] Marc Fisher, In Tunisia Act of One Fruit Vendor Sparks Wave of Revolution through the Arab World, *Washington Post*, March 26, 2011

hasn't necessarily led to an improvement[127] in the material position of these protesting citizens, but they did challenge the status quo by bringing down certain autocrats.

In 2011, the US saw its own anti-status quo movement with the Occupy[128] protests against government corruption that coincided with similar protests in everywhere from Nigeria[129] to Chile[130] and the Philippines[131]; meanwhile politicians in India and Nepal were even getting slapped by citizens so frustrated with government inaction.[132]

In 2012, we saw massive movements in the EU against their governments' austerity policies, particularly in Greece[133] and

---

[127] Shane Dixon Kavanaugh and Gilad Shiloach, Arab Spring Aftermath: More Conflict, Instability in the Middle East, *Vocativ*, Jan 25, 2016

[128] Maha Hosain Aziz, What Are the Occupiers Really Fighting For? *CNN*, April 18, 2012

[129] Gillian Parker, Nigeria Paralyzed by "Occupy" Protests Over Gas Prices, *Time*, Jan 9, 2012

[130] Chile Protests: Al Jazeera's Faul Lines Follows Student Movement, *Huffington Post*, Jan 4, 2012

[131] Occupy Protest in Manila, Philippines – In Pictures, *Guardian*, Dec 7, 2011

[132] Paul Mason, *Why It's Kicking Off Everywhere: The New Global Revolutions*, Verso Books, 2011

[133] Elinda Labropoulou, Thousands Protest Austerity Measures in Greece, *CNN*, Sept 26, 2012

Spain[134] that persisted[135] through 2018[136]. Yes, it didn't instantly lead to an immediate change in policy but citizens made their disappointment clear. In 2013, the mass protest movement in Egypt against President Mohammed Morsi led to his ouster[137], as it did in Thailand with the removal of Prime Minister Yingluck[138] Shinawatra by 2014.

Around this time, citizens began their anti-government protests[139] in Venezuela that have bled into today's major legitimacy crisis[140] and the Euromaidan protests ousted[141]

134 Raphael Minder, Tens of Thousands Protest Austerity in Spain, *New York Times*, May 13, 2012

135 Holly Ellyatt and Silvia Amaro, Are We Witnessing the End of Austerity – and What Does That Mean for Europe? *CNBC*, Dec 5, 2018

136 Phoebe Fronista, For Greece's Austerity-Hit Elderly, Bailout "Will Never End", Aug 17, 2018

137 Egypt Protests: Mass Celebrations in Cairo As President Morsi Ousted in Coup, *Telegraph*, 2013

138 Bangkok Tense As 100,000 Protesters Rally Against Yingluck Shinawatra's Adminstration, *ABC*, Nov 24, 2013

139 What Lies Behind the Protests in Venezuela? *BBC*, Mar 2, 2014

140 Pia Riggirozzi, Venezuela Is Putting Democracy and Its Legitimacy to Test, *The Conversation*, Feb 14, 2019

141 Sam Frizell, Ukraine Protesters Seize Kiev As President Flees, *Time*, Feb 22, 2014

President Yanukovych in Ukraine. In 2015, citizen protests[142] targeted President Dilma Rousseff in Brazil that led to her impeachment[143] and eventually led to far right populist Jair Bolsanaro's victory.

And of course in 2016 we saw many British citizens effectively vote[144] against the political status quo with the Brexit referendum, while their American counterpart voted for President Trump. This was followed by major movements against government corruption which led to the ouster of leaders in South Korea[145] by 2017 and Malaysia[146] by 2018[147]. On and off from 2013 into 2018, students have demanded education reform through

---

[142] Bruce Douglas, Brazilian President Under Fire As Tens of Thousands Protest in 200 Cities, *Guardian*, Aug 15, 2015

[143] Simon Romero, Dilma Rouseff Is Ousted As Brazil's President in Impeachment Vote, *New York Times*, Aug 31, 2016

[144] Maha Hosain Aziz, British PM Theresa May Faces a Rocky Road Ahead, *Observer*, Aug 2016

[145] South Korea's Presidential Scandal, *BBC*, Apr 6, 2018

[146] Editorial Board, Malaysia's Arrest of a Corrupt Politician Is a Step Toward Justice, *Washington Post*, July 4, 2018

[147] Vanessa Romo, Former South Korea President Sentenced to 8 More Years in Prison, *NPR*, July 20, 2018

protests[148] in Chilean cities, while anti-government sentiment has surged[149] against judicial reform in Poland. The year 2019 has seen more of the same, including citizen protests challenging the re-election plans for leaders in Sudan (75-year old Omar al-Bashir[150] who gave in and handed over leadership of the party[151]) and Algeria (82-year old Abdelaziz Bouteflika[152] who also succumbed to the pressure).

These are just a handful of examples of citizens challenging the political status quo – there are more globally. There's no question that for now, the greatest challenge for most political leaders and governments will continue to be how to regain the confidence of an increasingly angry citizenry such that they can effectively govern. This crisis of political legitimacy globally has

---

[148] Chile's Students Launch First Protest Under Pinera Adminstration, *Reuters*, Apr 19, 2018

[149] Poland Protests: Thousands Rally Against Court Changes, *BBC*, July 27, 2018

[150] Mohammed Alamin and Mike Cohen, Why Protests Are Raging Against Sudan's Leader, *Washington Post*, Mar 6, 2019

[151] Sudan's President Bashir Steps Down As Ruling Party Leader, *Al Jazeera*, Mar 1, 2019

[152] Algeria's Bouteflika Warns of 'Chaos' Ahead of Protests Against Him, *BBC*, Mar 7, 2019

deepened in recent years with no clear explanation or solution. The silver lining might be the emergence of new political actors who are from outside the mainstream, from US Congresswoman Alexandria Ocasio-Cortez[153] to El Savador's new president Nayib Bukele[154] and Botswana's youngest MP Bogolo Kenewendo.[155] It's too soon to say whether this will lead to sustained political change of course.

But again, *why* are citizens so angry? There are different reasons in each case, from high-level government corruption to rising inflation and flawed judicial reforms. The larger question to consider is why governments are being challenged *more* by citizens now than in previous decades. It partly boils down to tech.

HOW TECH HAS CREATED A CHRONIC CRISIS OF POLITICAL LEGITIMACY

[153] Benjamin Soloway, Power to the People, *Foreign Policy*, Winter 2019

[154] Merlin Delcid and Jack Guy, The Strange Political Path of Nayib Bukele, El Salvador's New President, *CNN*, Feb 10, 2019

[155] Nontobeko Mlambo, Botswana: Meet Botswana's Youngest Minister, Bogolo Kenewendo, *AllAfrica*, Apr 6, 2018

One reason citizens are more unhappy with their governments is because they are more *informed* about what governments are doing or not doing – this is of course in part because of tech[156]. There is simply more information for citizens to consume, whether it's the 24 hour news cycle, Facebook posts, blogs and even Tweets of world leaders. Real news or fake news, it doesn't seem to make a difference – access to more information and more opinions has made it that much easier for the average citizen to be more knowledgeable or at least be more critical of their governments.

Obviously, countries with limited Internet access and/or blocked social media are less likely to have such empowered citizens who are critical of their governments (you can guess the usual suspects). And more than four billion people[157], mostly in developing countries, don't even have Internet access. Still, the

---

[156] Maha Hosain Aziz, Democracy or Dictatorship, Does It Even Matter Anymore?, *Huffington Post*, Aug 7, 2017

[157] Emma Luxton, Four Billion People Still Don't Have Internet Access. Here's How to Connect Them, May 11, 2016

human right[158] of having access to tech, the Internet in particular, has played a key role in enlightening the average citizen in many countries such that he or she is more critical of government.

Tech has of course also allowed the more informed and reactionary citizen to be more *activist* against government. The Arab Spring was named the Facebook Revolution[159] after all. Social media has allowed for frustrated citizens to mobilize quicker to challenge governments when their expectation of their leaders has not been met. For instance, in Zimbabwe, youth used social media on their smartphones[160] to criticize[161] former President Robert Mugabe's 37-year rule – #ThisFlag[162] created a movement for change that ultimately contributed to his ouster.

---

[158] UN, The Promotion, Protection and Enjoyment of Human Rights on the Internet, *Human Rights Council*, June 27, 2016

[159] Jessi Hempel, Social Media Made the Arab Spring But Couldn't Save It, *Wired*, Jan 26, 2016

[160] Maeve Shearlaw, Armed with Smartphones And Memes, Zimbabwe's Protesters Find Their Voice Online, July 11, 2016

[161] Bruce Mutsvairo, Can Robert Mugabe Be Tweeted Out of Power?, July 26, 2016

[162] Daily Maverick, The Man Behind #ThisFlag, Zimbabwe's Accidental Movement For Change, May 26, 2016

In some cases, citizens even pushed their government to backtrack on certain policies thanks to social media-arranged protests – it didn't work with the movement against the controversial contraception law[163], but the Polish presidency did bow to protesters' demands[164] on judicial reforms. So thanks to tech, citizens are more informed, reactionary and activist. But this has also facilitated the more rapid decline of state-society relations as citizens seem to be challenging their leaders, governments or certain policies more often.

Whether we like it or not, we are headed towards – or need to move towards – a new type of political system. Any legitimate government today, in the democratic or nondemocratic context, needs to account for a more informed, activist, tech-savvy citizenry. It may be time to redesign the social contract between citizen and government.

---

163 Sofia Lotto Persio, Contraception in Poland: Government Pushes Ahead with Law Restricting Access to Morning After Pill, *Newsweek*, May 17, 2017

164 Agnieszka Barteczko and Pawel Florkiewicz, Polish President Halts Justice Reforms After Days of Protests, July 24, 2017

In fact, it may also be time to consider more urgently how tech can empower more governments to be more responsive to citizen expectation on a more regular basis; let's repair the strained relationship between citizen and state. Otherwise we can only expect to see more frustrated citizens throwing food at elected officials, slapping their politicians, setting themselves on fire outside state offices, protesting against specific policies and even bringing down more governments in countries around the world.

TECH CURE: A NEW SOCIAL CONTRACT BETWEEN CITIZEN AND GOVERNMENT LEVERAGING TECH?

Yes, partly *because* of tech, the average citizen globally is more informed (or at least has the opportunity to be more informed) about what his government is doing or even thinking of doing (thanks to certain presidential tweets). And again, partly *because* of tech, the average citizen is also more activist against government, leveraging social media to organize protest movements. This is one reason for the global crisis of political legitimacy we have witnessed recurrently since 2010.

This strained relationship between citizens and government in many democracies and nondemocracies effectively means the *social contract*[165] is broken. But perhaps leveraging tech could also help repair this key relationship? It may be time to consider how tech, in very precise ways, could be built into a new social contract for renewed political legitimacy in many countries globally.

First, what is the social contract? It boils down to the *expectation* that citizens have of their government. But what is it exactly that citizens expect? Well, it varies. The demands from citizen protesters are worth examining. Put simply, when these citizens protest, they are effectively saying certain expectations of government have not been met.

For instance, in Morocco[166], South Korea and Brazil[167], it is clear that citizens expect their governments to operate free of

[165] Maha Hosain Aziz, Time for a New Social Contract? *Huffington Post*, Aug 25, 2017

[166] Evelyn Nieves, Fighting for Basic Rights in Morocco, *New York Times*, July 27, 2017

[167] Thousands in Brazil Protest Gutting of Anticorruption Measures, *New York Times*, Apr 12, 2016

corruption; when they felt their government was corrupt, they protested. In various EU countries, including Spain[168] and Greece[169], citizens expect a policy that doesn't take away their benefits; when they felt their government's austerity policies were impacting their basic subsistence, they protested. If a government today wants to regain legitimacy in the eyes of its jaded population, it needs to recognize the *expectation* of its citizens as early as possible.

In fact, tech could be leveraged by government to determine the growing expectation of its more informed, empowered, tech-savvy citizenry on a more regular basis – ideally before citizens feel the need to repeatedly challenge the legitimacy of their leaders through protest. By collecting and analyzing big data of citizens online (e.g. through their social media and online searches), governments could understand their citizens' needs

[168] Reuters, Spain: Anti-Austerity Protest Attracts Thousands, *Euronews*, Dec 18, 2016

[169] James Edgar, Thousands Gather for Athens Anti-Austerity Protest, *Euronews*, Feb 21, 2017

better[170]. Critics of course rightly argue governments could use such tech as a way to monitor and even control citizens[171] that infringes on their rights, just as they could limit access to the Internet to stifle dissent (recent examples include Zimbabwe[172] and Russia[173]). It's not so clear cut and the revised social contract would have to take this valid concern into account.

Second, today's more informed, tech-empowered citizen clearly wants to have more dialogue with government, especially on contentious issues – and tech can help. Yes, we all know about President Trump's tweets[174] and he isn't the only world leader using this form of public communication with citizens (e.g. Canadian Prime Minister Justin Trudeau, Indian Prime Minister

[170] Eillie Anzilotti, This Plan For An AI-Based Direct Democracy Outsources Votes To A Predictive Algorithm, *Fast Company*, Apr 12, 2018

[171] Yuval Noah Harari, Why Technology Favors Tyranny, *The Atlantic*, Oct 2018

[172] Daniella Cheslow, Zimbabwe Orders Second Internet Shutdown In A Week Of Deadly Protests, *NPR*, Jan 18, 2019

[173] Russia Internet Freedom: Thousands Protest Against Cyber-Security Bill, *BBC*, Mar 10, 2019

[174] Vivian Salama, Trump Tweets Send Advisers Scrambling to Reshape Policy, *Boston Globe*, Aug 3, 2017

Narendra Modi); his 58.9 million followers can hear exactly what he is thinking and in theory can respond with a tweet.

It's important to note that half the world's population is already engaging with government online; countries like Estonia[175] are leading the way in e-governance[176] with citizens doing almost every municipal or state service online in mere minutes; there are also growing numbers of startups (e.g. CityBase in Chicago[177]) making certain government services more accessible to citizens. This is all progress towards (re)building citizens' trust[178] in government, easing the recurring crisis of political legitimacy.

Still, tech needs to be more central to the new social contract so the average citizen can interact with government much more often, *especially* on contentious issues. Let's use tech so citizens can ask about policies relating to sensitive issues like corruption and austerity; citizens should have more opportunity to

---

[175] We Have Built a Digital Society And So Can You, https://e-estonia.com/

[176] Innar Liiv, Welcome To E-Estonia, The Tiny Nation That's Leading Europe In Digital Innovation, Apr 4, 2017

[177] Utsav Gandhi, This Chicago Startup Is Changing How Governments Interact With Citizens, *Chicago Inno*, July 6, 2017

[178] Embracing Innovation in Government: Global Trends, *OECD*, Feb 2017

engage with government on their policy concerns more regularly and should be able to expect a direct, timely response. (And if not, MIT's César Hidalgo[179] argues for bypassing the politician through a personalized AI representative that can participate directly in democratic decisions and is based on citizens' preferences.)

Third, today's more informed, activist, tech-savvy citizen wants to have more input on policy – again, tech can help. Citizens have protested against specific policies like austerity in the EU for a few years – maybe it's time to get their ideas on what might work better? Yes, this can of course backfire when the average citizen isn't as informed as we hope (e.g. the Brexit referendum saw voters Googling[180] "what is the EU" hours after leaving it). But crowdsourcing tech – i.e. using the wisdom of an informed crowd of citizens to help make certain policy[181] – could be one way to

---

[179] César Hidalgo, A Bold Idea to Replace Politicians, TED2018

[180] Jeff John Roberts, Brits Scramble to Google "What is the EU?" Hours After Voting to Leave It, *Fortune*, June 24, 2016

[181] Tanja Aitamurto, Crowdsourcing for Democracy: New Era in Policy-Making, Committee for the Future, *Parliament of Finland*, 2012

make some policymaking more inclusive and reduce the legitimacy gap.

This technological approach to domestic policymaking was attempted in Iceland with its constitution[182] – over 50 percent of the population offered their views through Facebook and Twitter. It didn't quite work out the way we hoped[183], but it's a start. It did, however, work in Finland[184] with the passage of a new law – yes, it was just a non-controversial, off-road traffic law in a relatively stable country, but the point is it worked.[185]

Let's put some academics, experts and PhD researchers to work to determine what worked there before we consider how it might apply to policymaking in other countries where tensions between government and citizens are notably high. Crowdsourcing could be an innovative way to start to rebuild the relationship

---

[182] Harvey Morris, Crowdsourcing Iceland's Constitution, *New York Times*, Oct 24, 2012

[183] Haroon Siddique, Mob Rule: Iceland Crowdsources Its Next Constitution, *Guardian*, June 9, 2011

[184] Orion Jones, Crowdsourcing Legislation in Finland, *Big Think*, Oct 26, 2012

[185] Tanja Aitamurto, Helene Landemore, David Lee and Ashish Goel, Seven Lessons From the Crowdsourced Law Reform in Finland, *GovLab Blog*, Oct 30, 2013

between state and society in a new social contract in the coming years. It could be one way to ease our global crisis of political legitimacy.

This will be a hard sell in most countries – why would ruling elites want to make policymaking *more* inclusive?[186] It would in one sense take away from their own power or from their ability to please a small elite (or the "winning coalition"[187]) that can keep them in power. And obviously this wouldn't work in a country, say like Russia, where there are no immediate plans to democratize and protests can be quashed rather quickly.

But it might be a useful tool in democracies like postwar Sri Lanka where some minority groups (e.g. Tamils) may still feel disconnected from the majoritarian government.[188] It could also be a useful tool in countries where citizens repeatedly have singled out one policy they feel simply doesn't work – think of austerity

---

[186] Maha Hosain Aziz, The Rise of Anti-Government Protests Around the World and How to Reduce It in 2015, *Huffington Post*, Dec 31, 2014

[187] Bruce Bueno de Mesquita and Alastair Smith, *The Dictator's Handbook: Why Bad Behavior Is Almost Always Good Politics*, Public Affairs, 2011

[188] Iain Marlow and Anusha Ondaatjie, Why Sri Lanka Risks Return to Violence, *Washington Post*, Dec 13, 2018

policies in EU countries or sensitive anti-corruption laws in Brazil.[189] If we asked the Tamil minority for their input on the development agenda in former conflict-hit areas in the north, anti-austerity protesters in Spain for their input on economic policies or anti-corruption protesters in Brazil, would that help reduce anti-government sentiment? Would this help ease the legitimacy crisis so leaders might better govern? No question it's worth looking into even if there are sensitivities surrounding this. At the very least, it could help with the psychology of the average citizen such that they would feel their voice is heard by government.

Yet even if this is attempted, who will implement such crowdsourcing tech? If individual governments can't manage it, even with its recurring legitimacy[190] challenges[191] the UN is a logical back-up. The organization has a renewed focus on using tech to do everything from assessing damage caused by natural

[189] Maha Hosain Aziz, How Crowdsourcing Anti-Corruption Policy Might Ease Brazil's Legitimacy Crisis, *Huffington Post*, Aug 25, 2015

[190] Charles W. Yost, The United Nations: Crisis of Confidence and Will, *Foreign Affairs*, Oct 1966

[191] Séverine Autesserre, The Crisis of Peacekeeping: Why the UN Can't End Wars, *Foreign Affairs*, Jan/Feb 2019

disasters to generating anti-poverty goals from youth in the next development agenda and overcoming language barriers with refugees globally.[192]

There's a lot to figure out. But the bottom line – the social contract has been broken for awhile now. Whether we like it or not, any government today, in the democratic *or* nondemocratic context, needs to account for a more informed, activist, tech-savvy citizenry. It also needs to leverage tech for renewed political legitimacy. This basic truth must be embedded in a revised social contract for the 21st century.

TECH CURE: BLOCKCHAIN
TO REDUCE GOVERNMENT CORRUPTION

One recurring reason globally for citizen frustration against most governments is corruption. It has contributed to the crisis of political legitimacy. Again, consider the anti-corruption protest movements in Brazil in 2015–2016 and in South Korea in 2016–2017 that ultimately led to the ouster of both presidents, Dilma

---

[192] UN Secretary-General's Strategy on New Technologies, Sept 2018

Rousseff and Park Geun-hye, respectively. In Latin America, Peruvians challenged the administration of Martin Vizcarra about systemic corruption[193] following reports of judges accepting bribes. In the Middle East, Iraqis' anti-corruption protests led to the ouster[194] of one allegedly corrupt minister with links to fake contracts. In Africa, Kenyans (especially youth[195]) protested corruption scandals involving missing public funds. In Europe, Slovakia's citizens demanded more resignations over government corruption[196], even after their protests brought down the prime minister. And so on. A major struggle for political leaders continues to be how to regain the confidence of a very suspicious citizenry such that they can effectively govern – and of course tackle corruption itself.

---

[193] Simeon Tegel, Corruption Scandals Have Ensnared Three Peruvian Presidents: Now the whole political system could change, *Washington Post*, Aug 12, 2018

[194] Iraq's Electricity Minister Fired After Weeks of Protests, *DW*, July 29, 2018

[195] Max Bearak, Kenyans Have Had It with Corruption: Their leaders may finally be doing something about it, *Washington Post*, July 17, 2018

[196] Tatiana Jancarikova, Slovak Protesters Demand More Resignations Over Corruption Neglect, *Reuters*, Apr 15, 2018

Tech, specifically blockchain[197], could be *one[198]* way to repair the strained citizen-government relationship while *also* reducing[199] corruption[200]. Yes, this simple technology – a digital ledger in which transactions can be recorded chronologically, transparently and in a decentralized system – was first created in 2009 to track bitcoin. But it could also be precisely what governments[201] need to help restore citizen trust and ease the legitimacy crisis. Blockchain would mean all financial transactions involving public funds would be traceable, in theory reducing the chance of government corruption.

In fact, some governments[202] are already testing out this technology, including in countries known for endemic corruption.

---

197 Maha Hosain Aziz, #3 Could Blockchain Ease Governments' Chronic Legitimacy Crises? *Medium*, Aug 3, 2018

198 Promise and Peril: Blockchain, Bitcoin and the Fight Against Corruption, *Transparency International*, Jan 31, 2018

199 Eduardo Aldaz Carroll, Can Cryptocurrencies and Blockchain Help Fight Corruption?, *World Bank*, Feb 20, 2018

200 Carlos Santiso, Can Blockchain Help in the Fight Against Corruption?, *World Economic Forum*, Mar 12, 2018

201 Carlos Santiso, Will Blockchain Disrupt Government Corruption? *Stanford Innovation Social Review*, Mar 5, 2018

202 Nicky Woolf, What Could Blockchain Do for Politics? *Medium*, Jan 8, 2018

In Mexico, blockchain is being developed by the government to track[203] bids[204] for public contracts. In India, Andra Pradesh is the first state to use blockchain to manage land records in a country where over 65%[205] of civil cases are property-related. In Kenya and Nigeria, local startups are also exploring how blockchain could reduce corruption in land ownership.[206] And so on. Could blockchain restore citizen trust over time, ultimately easing governments' chronic legitimacy crises?

The good news is there is a lot of investment going into developing tech for government, i.e. *govtech*. At the first GovTech Summit in Paris in 2018, we were told that the $400 billion govtech industry will increase 15% a year over the next six

---

[203] Nick Tsakanikas, Mexico Aims to Eliminate Corruption in Public Tenders Using Blockchain Technology, *BitRates*, Aug 3, 2018

[204] David Floyd, Mexico Tests Blockchain to Track Public Contract Bids, Apr 5, 2018

[205] Sharanya Haridas, This Indian City Is Embracing BlockChain Technology -- Here's Why, *Forbes*, Mar 5, 2018

[206] Kevin Mwanza and Henry Wilkins, African Startups Bet On Blockchain to Tackle Land Fraud, *Reuters*, Feb 16, 2018

years.[207] This summit included political leaders, entrepreneurs and investors discussing how startups and new tech can improve public services and democratic practices. This is undoubtedly progress towards reducing that legitimacy gap between citizen and governments creatively through tech.

So Reader, you tell me… Is democracy still the best system of government? If not, what should replace it? I suggest tech might be part of our future government – and the future has clearly already begun. But what do you think?

---

[207] Nick Ismail, GovTech to Hit $1 Trillion By 2025, *Information Age*, Nov 12, 2018

CHAPTER 4

ECONOMIC CRISIS

ECONOMIC RISKS AND THE GLOBALIZATION CHALLENGE: FROM CITIZEN MOVEMENTS TO POPULIST GOVERNMENTS

Public intellectuals like economist Nouriel Roubini rightly warn us that the "perfect storm" is upon us and will stall global growth through 2020.[208] The IMF's Christine Lagarde has downgraded global growth as well[209]. These negative economic predictions will likely persist, particularly as the US-China trade war hovers over us – perhaps the greatest risk to the global economy.[210] In fact, tech billionaire Jack Ma warns this trade war

---

[208] Roubini Warns of 'Perfect Storm' Stalling Global Growth in 2020, *Bloomberg Surveillance TV Show*, Sept 7, 2018

[209] Lori Ioannou, IMF Chair Christine Lagarde Cuts Global Growth Forecast for 2019 to 3.5 Percent, *CNBC*, Jan 22, 2019

[210] Sam Meredith, Trump's Trade War with China Is 'the Biggest Risk to the Global Economy,' BlackRock Exec Says, *CNBC*, Sept 4, 2018

(which he also calls the "most stupid thing") could last "two decades".[211]

All of this exists in the backdrop of a growing techonomic cold war between the US and China[212] especially over AI (note: AI expert Lee[213] gives China the edge), 5G[214] and how data[215] itself is used in different regions. We are likely headed for the fracturing[216] of the global internet which, over time, will be a destabilizing factor for our geopolitics, politics, economy and society in ways we don't fully understand yet.[217]

---

[211] Bloomberg, Jack Ma Says Trade War Is the 'Most Stupid Thing' as U.S.-China Tensions Boil, *Time*, Nov 5, 2018

[212] Ian Bremmer and Cliff Kupchan, Risk 3: Global Tech Cold War, *Top Risks for 2018 Report*, Eurasia Group, 2018

[213] Eamon Barrett, Ex-Google Exec Kai-Fu Lee Says China Is Winning the Race to Implement AI, *Fortune*, Nov 29, 2019

[214] Jansen Tham, Why 5G Is the Next Front of US-China Competition, *Diplomat*, Dec 13, 2018

[215] Kieran O'Hara and Wendy Hall, Four Internets: The Geopolitics of Digital Governance, *Centre for International Governance Innovation*, CIGI Paper No. 206, Dec 7, 2018

[216] Wendy Hall, The Internet Risks Fracturing Into Quarters, *Financial Times*, Dec 11, 2018

[217] Maha Hosain Aziz, What Are the Global Risks to Watch in 2019?, *Medium*, Jan 9, 2019

Alas, there's one piece of good news for our economic situation: the International Labor Organization reports global unemployment is at its lowest level since the 2008 global economic crisis. But the concern persists about a *youth* unemployment[218] crisis. Even if the youth unemployment rate has reduced a bit, it is still three times higher than the adult rate worldwide.[219] This is a concern.

Besides such growing economic risks, the reality is the global economic status quo of *globalization* has been challenged for awhile. This is another part of our unique global legitimacy crisis. Yes, many world leaders, including China's President Xi Jinping since the 2017 World Economic Forum at Davos[220], and international institutions[221] like the IMF, still defend globalization.

[218] Margaret Besheer, ILO Fights Global Youth Unemployment Crisis, *Voice of America*, Feb 2, 2016

[219] World Employment and Social Outlook: Trends 2019, *ILO*, Feb 13, 2019

[220] Max Ehrenfreund, World Leaders Find Hope for Globalization in Davos Amid Populist Revolt, *Washington Post*, Jan 17, 2017

[221] Martin Crutsinger and Paul Wiseman, Leaders of IMF and World Bank Defend Globalization, *US News*, Apr 20, 2017

But let's face it – globalization has been challenged for almost 20 years.

First, it was *citizens* who spoke out. They felt excluded from globalization's expected benefits and launched movements[222] like the Battle Against Seattle and Carnival against Capitalism in 1999, while protests recurred outside other WTO[223], G7 and G20[224] meetings in the years since.

But something has shifted. The citizen-led movement evolved in the last decade into a political force that cannot be ignored. Now we see *governments* themselves have responded to these frustrated citizens by promoting an anti-globalization agenda rooted in *populism*[225], in parts of the EU[226], Latin America[227] and

---

[222] A Brief History of the Anti-Globalization Movement, *DW*, June 7, 2017

[223] Noah Smith, The Dark Side of Globalization: Why Seattle's 1999 Protesters Were Right, *The Atlantic*, Jan 6, 2014

[224] Scott Neuman, Anti-Globalization Protests Spark Violence In Hamburg For Second Day, *NPR*, July 7, 2017

[225] Marc Champion, The Rise of Populism, *Bloomberg*, Jan 22, 2019

[226] William A. Galston, Rise of European Populism and the Collapse of the Center-Left, *Brookings Institution*, Mar 8, 2018

[227] Robert Muggah and Brian Winter, Is Populism Making a Comeback in Latin America? *Foreign Policy*, Oct 23, 2017

of course the US. The economic status quo of globalization is clearly under threat. The problem is the proposed alternative of populism may not necessarily deliver what citizens expect either. This may over time manifest itself in citizen frustration at *both* ends of the spectrum – protests will recur against globalization but ultimately may also surface against populism, as all types of governments struggle to meet citizens' economic expectation.

What's also concerning is that the anti-globalization backlash we've been witnessing in recent years looks eerily similar[228] to the events in the years leading up to World War I. This period was often termed the first era of globalization, which also led to populism, major conflicts and a depression. What does this mean for us today – is our current situation simply history repeating itself? It's difficult to say with absolute certainty.

What *is* clear is that the larger *moral economy[229]* is breaking. Theorists have historically used moral economy rhetoric

---

[228] Ana Swanson, The World Today Looks Ominously Like It Did Before World War I, *Washington Post*, Dec 29, 2016

[229] Maha Hosain Aziz #4 Time to Rebuild Our Moral Economy? Tech May Be Key., *Medium*, Oct 14, 2018

to explain rural movements where protesters felt their right to a basic subsistence was being threatened by elites. Today, whether it's about populism, a broader challenge to globalization or the rejection of a particular policy, many citizens globally are challenging their governments over economic conditions which haven't met their expectation.

Effectively, an informal contract has weakened between governments and citizens involving citizens' right to a basic subsistence – however they define it. Now if you also throw in the looming tech cloud of automation unemployment, this is cause for even more anxiety. It may be time to rebuild our moral economy. We must consider what economic expectations we have of our governments?

HOW TECH IS INCREASING ECONOMIC RISK: AUTOMATION UNEMPLOYMENT & THE RISE OF THE PRECARIATS

We have all heard about the threat of automation at this point. How do we prepare ourselves for the fact that robots *will* take away certain jobs[230] in industries like manufacturing, retail and transport? In fact, it's already started and it will just keep coming at us. There are umpteen studies and recent empirical examples to reiterate this. According to expert Lee[231], AI will replace 40% of jobs over the next 15 years[232] (of course, he also reassures us how certain jobs requiring empathy, creativity and compassion will be safe[233], e.g. psychiatry, teaching, fiction writing, management and criminal defense law). A McKinsey report echoes this sentiment, highlighting that all countries, both developed and developing, will experience this shift at some point.[234] Over 50 percent of work activities will be automated in

---

[230] In some cases though, robots are actually making jobs better for workers, according to a joint research project by McKinsey and the World Economic Forum on "lighthouse" factories (White Paper: Fourth Industrial Revolution Beacons of Technology and Innovation in Manufacturing, Jan 2019).

[231] Dan Robitzski, Former Google Exec: AI Will Replace 40% of Jobs in 15 Years, *Futurism*, Jan 10, 2019

[232] Don Reisinger, AI Expert Says Automation Could Replace 40% of Jobs in 15 Years, *Fortune*, Jan 10, 2019

[233] Kai-Fu Lee, 10 Jobs That Are Safe in an AI World, *Medium*, Oct 1, 2018

[234] James Manyika, Michael Chui, Mehdi Miremadi, Jacques Bughin, Katy George, Paul Willmott, and Martin Dewhurst, Harnessing Automation for a Future That Works, *McKinsey Global Institute*, Jan 2017

places like Kenya, Morocco, Peru, Colombia, Mexico, Costa Rica, Czech Republic, Turkey, Japan, Thailand and Qatar.[235]

Are governments prepared for the unemployment that goes hand in hand with such automation? It doesn't feel like it. As tech billionaire Ma put it, automation will create "more pain than happiness in the next 30 years"[236] due to unemployment. Of course, it is not an easy task to prepare us for – apparently 80% of the jobs people will pursue in 2030 have not even been created yet.[237] So what should be done? There is definitely a *very* public push by all governments[238] to commit to tech, especially AI, with major policy announcements from the[239] US[240] to Japan and

[235] Michael Chui, James Manyika and Mehdi Miremadi, The Countries Most (and Least) Likely to be Affected by Automation, *Harvard Business Review*, Apr 12, 2017

[236] Olivia Solon, Alibaba Founder Jack Ma: AI Will Cause People 'More Pain Than Happiness', *Guardian*, Apr 24, 2017

[237] Jason Hiner, When 85% of the Jobs of 2030 Haven't Been Created Yet, How Do You Prepare?, *Tech Republic*, May 23, 2018

[238] Tim Dutton, An Overview of National Strategies, *Medium*, June 28, 2018

[239] Tim Simonite, Trump's Plan to Keep America First in AI, *Wired*, Feb 11, 2019

[240] New Strategy Outlines Path Forward for AI, US Department of Defense, Feb 2019

Canada[241] recurrently since 2017; naturally all governments want to remain economically competitive and relevant to the global market.

But economists[242], like Lukas Schlogl and Andy Sumner, worry that most governments are in fact not focused on the *effect* of this shift on citizens. Governments are more focused on surviving major legitimacy challenges, overcoming economic weakness and other domestic issues – preparing citizens for possible future unemployment is not an immediate concern. So what's next for the average citizen; what should we expect of our role in an increasingly tech-oriented economy?

According to World Economic Forum Founder Klaus Schwab, today we already see many *precariats*[243], i.e. those who are not sure of how they will survive as they get older. This label

---

[241] Hiawatha Bray, Justin Trudeau Boasts AI in Talk at MIT, *Boston Globe*, May 18, 2018

[242] Lukas Schlogl and Andy Sumner, The Rise of the Robot Reserve Army: Automation and the Future of Economic Development, Work, and Wages in Developing Countries, *Center for Global Development*, Working Paper 487, July 2, 2018

[243] Arjun Kharpal, Davos Founder: World 'Identity Crisis' Driven By Globalization Has Led to Trump's Election, Brexit, *CNBC*, Feb 12, 2017

of the precariat with limited occupational identity could apply to Generation Z, Baby Boomers, and well, possibly everyone in between. SOAS economist Guy Standing coined this term in his book of the same name,[244] revealing that precariats are the new global class with "no occupational identity or narrative to give to their lives."[245] He rightly argues "this creates existential insecurity, and goes with the fact that for the first time in history many people have education above the level of labour they can expect to obtain."

This person "lives in economic uncertainty, usually in chronic unsustainable debt, in which one shock, mistaken decision or illness could tip them over the edge." That is a lot of anxiety already building in individual precariats. Now throw in the looming cloud of automation unemployment in an uncertain world order, where democracy itself is under threat and most governments are muddling along post-economic crisis. What does

---

[244] Guy Standing, *The Precariat: A New Dangerous Class*, Bloomsbury, 2016

[245] Guy Standing, Meet the Precariat, the New Global Class Fueling the Rise of Populism, *World Economic Forum*, Nov 9, 2016

this mean for the precariat class – or rather, how many *more* precariats will emerge from those millions of people globally who will lose their jobs to automation?

Again, we are not sufficiently prepared for what's coming. We know digital skills are key for our future economy and the Fourth Industrial Revolution[246] means new jobs will be created[247]; but where does that leave those of us who for whatever reason may *not* be able to adapt? Maybe more entrepreneurship will be key to give more precariats a sense of purpose; or perhaps UBI will appease this growing class, as is being debated these days. But for now, many will have to tackle a work-related *identity crisis* which will add to the anxiety we *already* feel amid our global legitimacy crisis. It doesn't appear there is a sustained policy focus by governments to tackle the psychological toll of existing unemployment, let alone the toll that will come with waves of *automation* unemployment.

---

[246] Sam Meredith, Carolin Roth, Fourth Industrial Revolution Expected to Boost Job Creation: CEOs, *CNBC*, Jan 18, 2017

[247] Arjun Kharpal, AI Will Create More Jobs That Can't Be Filled, Not Mass Unemployment, Alphabet's Eric Schmidt Says, *CNBC*, June 16, 2017

TECH CURES: A NEW MORAL *TECH* ECONOMY, CREATIVE UBI & JOB APPS

Well, what now, Reader? It's clearly a tough situation. We are all headed for a difficult few years, and even decades, professionally. The truth is many of us have *already* struggled post-2008 global economic crisis on the career front, losing our jobs and struggling to figure out where we fit in professionally. More of that is coming. It will be key for us to be more open to change and especially to learning new skills – or risk becoming precariats.

I've learned that in my own career and in many ways I'm still learning. As a PhD graduate in 2012, I, and many of my peers, dreamed of living the life of the full-time, tenured university professor, writing journal articles and books while we educated the next generation. It didn't quite work out like that for all of us. And we were forced to revisit and revise our dreams (I personally never thought I'd split my time between academia, consulting, blogging and comic book creating.)

I also never thought tech would be relevant to my career as an educator. But it has been thrust upon me – from teaching courses virtually to doing collaborative analytical research through crowdsourcing consulting online and leveraging open source data for my own book research. Again, we have no choice but to be open and adapt with a growth mindset.

At this sensitive global turning point, it's crucial to urgently consider what steps we can take going forward to be productive members of our evolving tech economies. I want to suggest a few possible cures to ease this growing challenge to the economic status quo. Above all, we need to consider the average person and his or her role in the tech economy. We need to consider how we can prevent more people from becoming precariats before they fall through the cracks with no "occupational identity".

First, I suggest we revise our moral economy – or more appropriately a moral *tech* economy where citizen expectations are redefined for governments. Again, the moral economy refers to the informal contract between governments and citizens involving citizens' right to a basic subsistence – however they define it. It boils down to the economic expectations that citizens have of their governments.

But governments must be aggressive in explicitly engaging with citizens about what citizen expectations might be in a tech economy.[248] It's not enough to hear CEOs and tech billionaires warn us about automation unemployment. We need our *political leaders*[249] to *inform* us of this threat and explain how they will *help* us during this transition period. How *many* citizens will lose jobs and *when*? Will automation mean our expectations of a basic subsistence will not be met? The expectations embedded in a moral tech economy, involving the government and citizen (and perhaps

---

[248] Creating the Economy of the Future: How Cutting-Edge Economies Are Transforming Our World, Creating New Jobs – And Protecting Our Data Along the Way, *Wired,* Mar 2018

[249] It is worth noting there's one political actor – a US 2020 presidential candidate and fellow Brown alum named Andrew Yang – who recognizes the serious threat of automation unemployment. He is running on a platform of Universal Basic Income (UBI) which he feels is one way to prepare the US population for automation unemployment.

the tech firm as well), need to be defined now to reduce risks in the future.

Second, we need some kind of social provision during this sensitive period of automation unemployment. We keep hearing certain tech billionaires (e.g. Bill Gates[250]) chiming in with policy suggestions like UBI – basically give everyone a monthly stipend in case they lose their jobs to robots. A UBI project in Finland has already shown "no strings attached money" has, well, made people happier.[251] But is UBI affordable for most governments today? It seems tricky at this point given growing global and domestic economic risks.

So let's be creative about how to fund something like UBI for the automation unemployed if governments cannot foot the bill. Other tech billionaires (e.g. Richard Branson[252]) argue that part of the future "extreme wealth" of AI firms can fund UBI. Some

---

[250] Chris Weller, Bill Gates Says It's Too Early for Basic Income, But Over Time 'Countries Will Be Rich Enough", *Business Insider*, Feb 27, 2017

[251] Fast Company, The One Clear Result of Finland's Basic Income Trial: It Made People Happier, *Medium*, Feb 20, 2019

[252] Catherine Clifford, Billionaire Richard Branson: Extreme Wealth Generated By AI Industry Should Be Used For Cash Handouts, *CNBC*, Oct 10, 2010

experts call for UBI to be paid via a cryptocurrency[253] running on blockchain.[254] This has already been attempted by Grantcoin[255] even if the results are unclear. But it is worth revisiting to see if this is possible on a mass, global scale.

Another option involves the ongoing debate about tech companies using our data – for free. Let's be compensated[256] for this – or at least give those unemployed by automation the option to be compensated for their data in a "data-for-basic-income swap" with tech firms.[257] As the *Financial Times* put it, if data is "the new oil then we may have found a 21st-century revenue stream."[258]

253 Dom Galeon, Universal Basic Income Could Become a Reality, Thanks to This Technology: We Could Make This Happen, *Futurism*, Mar 10, 2017

254 Marc Howard, How to Start Universal Basic Income with Cryptocurrency, *Medium*, Aug 16, 2018

255 Grantcoin has seen been renamed Mannabase. Sara Bizarro, Basic Income Cryptocurrency Grantcoin, Upgrades and Name Change, *Basic Income Earth Network*, Aug 4 2017

256 will. i. am, We Need to Own Our Data as a Human Right – and Be Compensated For It, *Economist*, Jan 21, 2019

257 Jolene Creighton, Experts May Have a Viable Alternative to Universal Basic Income: A radical new idea could be the answer to automation, *Futurism*, Nov 8, 2017

258 John Thornhill of *Financial Times*, Why Facebook Should Pay US a Basic Income, *Medium*, Aug 8, 2017

We might even consider crowdfunding a basic income for those hit by automation-linked unemployment. Tech firms – or even certain charitable billionaires – could fund UBI initially (after all, an Egyptian billionaire[259] had offered to *buy* a Greek island back in 2015 to ease the Syrian refugee crisis[260]) Or maybe governments might simply ask citizens for help to crowdfund UBI initially (this was attempted by Malaysian Prime Minister Mahathir Mohamad with the Hope Fund to cover the country's huge debt[261] after a local law student started her own campaign[262]). Clearly, it is still worth exploring creative and *tech*-linked ways to fund UBI – or at least a basic income for those hit by automation-linked unemployment.

Third, there needs to be an aggressive, explicit effort to tackle the *psychological* toll of automation and related

---

[259] Maha Hosain Aziz, *The Global Kid: A Political Comic Book*, 2016

[260] Ivana Kottasova, Egyptian Billionaire Offers to Buy Island for Refugee, *CNN*, Sept 10, 2015

[261] Siobhán O'Grady, Malaysia Has $250 Billion of Debt. The Government is Trying to Crowdfund It, *Washington Post*, June 2, 2018

[262] Malaysian Starts Crowdfunding to Help Reduce Country's Debt, *Strait Times*, May 26, 2018

unemployment. It's not so straightforward to tell someone to just learn *new* skills so they can be part of this *new* economy. Our ego gets in the way. We attain a certain level of experience or professional status and assume we don't have to look for work anymore. We don't want to feel we are starting from scratch, as we get older. For those who don't instantly fit into the future tech economy, that period of being jobless will create anxiety.

Emotional support from psychologists is necessary for this specific type of joblessness. There are already very popular apps like New Zealand startup's[263] ThinkLadder[264] to treat mental health issues by changing the way people think – perhaps an app can be tailored specifically for the automation unemployed or to rewire them with a growth mindset to learn new skills in a new tech economy. I know, easier said than done, but one of many possible cures to explore.

---

[263] Disha Daswaney, This Brilliant App Is Launching in the UK to Help Support People with Anxiety, *Evening Standard*, Oct 24, 2017

[264] Sohni Mitter, Thinkladder Wants to Be the Pocket Therapist for Patients of Depression and Anxiety, *Your Story*, Sept 28, 2018

Fourth, we know new jobs will be created. But matching the unemployed with these new jobs will be key. Let's not leave the automated unemployed to figure it out on their own. There must be an aggressive, explicit public relations campaign led by tech firms and governments to show the unemployed they *have* the skills to work these new jobs – or can be taught.

One study suggests women[265] will have an edge in tech, especially AI, as they have the necessary emotional intelligence required, relative to men. Whether or not everyone agrees with that, encouraging women in a tech economy makes sense – apparently $12 trillion could be added to the global GDP by 2025 simply by advancing women's equality in the workplace.[266] Perhaps an app can be created that specifically caters to the automation unemployed? It can match the skills of the current workforce with those needed for new jobs in a tech economy. It

[265] Sarah O'Connor of *Financial Times*, The Robot-Proof Skills That Give Women an Edge in the Age of AI: Men are in danger of being left behind as future well-paid jobs may involve emotional intelligence, *Medium*, Feb 12, 2019

[266] Jonathan Woetzel, Anu Madgavkar, Kweilin Ellingrud, Eric Labaye, Sandrine Devillard, Eric Kutcher, James Manyika, Richard Dobbs, and Mekala Krishnan How Advancing Women's Equality Can Add $12 Trillion to Global Growth, *McKinsey Global Institute Report*, Sept 2015

can target women or a certain age group. Bottom line, it can match people's skills to new jobs and reduce that period of anxiety coming from unemployment. Again, easier said than done, of course, but it's an idea.

So Reader, time to recap:

If the status quo of globalization is being challenged, is populism the answer?

Are we prepared for the looming cloud of automation unemployment?

And more importantly, what about you – do you have an occupational identity or do you see yourself as a potential precariat losing your occupational identity in a tech economy? If so, let's do something about it.

CHAPTER 5

SOCIAL CRISIS

ARE YOU A GLOBALIST OR A NATIONALIST?

At this point in the book, it should be crystal clear to you, Reader – this is an unusually sensitive time in our human development. Frankly, what we are experiencing globally is unprecedented. Take a step back and reflect again for yourself. … We are really questioning everything – from the structure of our international system to our relationship with government and even the very nature of our work. But, in many ways, the greatest risk in our global legitimacy crisis is social. It's deeply *personal*. The greatest threat to our stability is the fact that we are also questioning *who we are*.

How do we define ourselves today?

What values[267] guide us?

---

[267] Maha Hosain Aziz, <u>What Are Our Global Values in Today's Post-Hegemonic World?</u>, *Huffington Post*, Aug 29, 2017

DR MAHA HOSAIN AZIZ

According to the WEF's Schwab, citizens everywhere continue to struggle with an identity crisis *because* of globalization – they cannot "digest" the "complexity of the world" and this causes "emotional turmoil."[268] He might be right. And yet the global identity crisis of today's post-hegemonic world is distinct requiring distinct solutions.

First, we must ask the key question – are we globalists or nationalists?[269] According to various studies, we are confused. A BBC poll[270] revealed that in recent years people have been identifying more as global citizens rather than national citizens, especially in emerging economies. Then again, as we all know, xenophobia – i.e. fear or hatred of the foreigner or simply the *other* – is very much on the rise[271], especially in developed economies. As UN Secretary-General António Guterres put it at the

---

[268] Arjun Kharpal, Davos Founder: World 'Identity Crisis' Driven By Globalization Has Led to Trump's Election, Brexit, *CNBC*, Feb 12, 2017

[269] Maha Hosain Aziz, Do We Understand the Global Identity Crisis of Today's Post-Hegemonic World?, *Huffington Post*, Sept 13, 2017

[270] Naomi Grimley, Identity 2016: 'Global Citizenship' Rising, Poll Suggests, *BBC*, Apr 28, 2016

[271] Simon Tisdall, Rise of Xenophobia Is Fanning Immigration Flames in EU and US, *Guardian*, June 22, 2018

40th session of the Human Rights Council in February 2019: "We are seeing a groundswell of xenophobia, racism and intolerance – including rising anti-Semitism and anti-Muslim hatred. ... Indeed, hate is moving into the mainstream – in liberal democracies and authoritarian states alike."[272]

He's right: this *is* sadly a global phenomenon. This distaste for the other has been bleeding deeper into societies around the world for a few years. Consider, for instance, the actions of empowered hate groups against[273] many[274] migrants[275] and refugees in the US[276] and in some European[277] countries.[278] Will

---

[272] Carrie Thompson, UN Security General Warns of Rise in Threats to Human Rights, *Jurist*, Feb 26, 2019

[273] European Islamophobia Report, 2015-2017

[274] Ericha Penzien, Xenophobic and Racist Hate Crimes Surge in the European Union, *Human Rights Brief*, Feb 8, 2017

[275] Jon Henley, Bus Seats Mistaken for Burqas By Members of Anti-Immigrant Group, *Guardian*, Aug 2, 2017

[276] Rage Against Change: Intelligence Report, Issue 166, *Southern Poverty Law Center*, Spring 2019

[277] Barry D. Wood, Storm Clouds of Nationalism Gather Over Eastern Europe, *Marketwatch*, Sept 5, 2017

[278] Vocativ, Refugees Fear Rising Anti-Muslim Backlash In Europe, *Huffington Post*, Jan 13, 2017

these minorities ever (re)gain a sense of belonging alongside the

majority? Perhaps, but probably not in the near term.

This xenophobic strain has of course also spilled over into

some governments[279] with their populist rhetoric[280]. At this point

it's unclear who will win this growing debate. A Deloitte

Millennial Survey[281] reveals more citizens, especially in developed

economies, are "pessimistic" about the social and political

direction of their countries. But what about you, Reader – are you a

globalist or a nationalist? We each need to decide this for

ourselves, as do our leaders.

Understanding how our global identity may be changing also

requires us to revisit our global values. What *are* they now? Or

maybe the more urgent question is, what *were* they? As you know,

democracy was *the* global value after the US won the Cold War

against the former Soviet Union. This gave the US government

---

[279] Steve Cannane, Geert Wilders, Dutch Right-Wing Politician, Pledges to "De-Islamise" the Netherlands Ahead of Election, *ABC Net*, March 12, 2017

[280] Katia Lopez Hodoyan, Denmark Approves Plan to Send Unwanted Migrants to "Virus" Island, *Al Jazeera*, Dec 20, 2018

[281] Pessimism Runs Rampant, Deloitte Millennial Survey, 2017

sufficient legitimacy in the 1990s to 2010s to promote democracy over all other ideologies, along with human rights, to the global community. This was a marker of the post-Cold War era.

But (as covered in Chapter 2 on the new world order,) the US role has changed, at least for now. Promoting[282] democracy and human rights does not appear to be a priority of the current[283] US government.[284] And in turn democracy and human rights may not necessarily be the most prominent global values anymore. But let's dig deeper. *Who* is deciding our global values now?

Well, there are so many influencers shaping our international system, from the non-US superpower to the aggressive smaller state, the tech-savvy citizen and certain public figures – and they still all believe in promoting democracy or human rights in some way. Germany's Chancellor Angela Merkel, for now the de-facto

---

[282] Tracy Wilkinson, Human Rights Fade from US Foreign Policy Agenda Under Trump, *LA Times*, Apr 5, 2017

[283] Jenna Johnson and Abigail Hauslohner, "I Think Islam Hates Us": A Timeline of Trump's Comments About Islam and Muslims, *Washington Post*, May 20, 2017

[284] Josh Rogin, US State Department Considers Dropping 'Democracy' From Its Mission Statement, *Independent*, Aug 1, 2017

leader[285] of the free world, seems to be taking a larger role in democracy promotion abroad. Smaller states like Canada[286], the Netherlands and Norway[287] are rising to the occasion to defend certain issues in global human rights. The tech-savvy citizen protester is more united globally on issues like women's rights[288], immigration[289] and climate change.[290]

And individuals with a public profile are also offering their two cents on global values. Consider actress America Ferrera[291] promoting activism through her advocacy organization Harness or actress and Special Envoy to the UN High Commissioner for Refugees Angelina Jolie who recently spoke of "equality for

[285] James P. Rubin, The Leader of the Free World Meets Donald Trump, *Politico*, Mar 16, 2017

[286] Kathleen Harris, Trudeau Touts Open Canadian Immigration System In Face of Trump Travel Ban, *CBC News*, June 27, 2017

[287] Jon Sharman, Norway Joins Dutch International Abortion Fund to Combat Donald Trump's Aid Ban, *Independent*, Feb 21, 2017

[288] Nosheen Iqbal, Women Around the World March Against Austerity and Violence, *Guardian*, Jan 19, 2019

[289] Chelsea Bailey and Katie Wong, Global Demonstrations Over Trump's Policies Heat Up Amid Anger Over Travel Ban, *NBC News*, Feb 4, 2017

[290] Luisa Beck, "We Don't Have Time Anymore": In face of climate change, young people across Europe are protesting for their future, Feb 15, 2019

[291] Rebecca Wilson, 25,000 People Just Watched America Ferrera Encourage a Culture of Activism, *Cosmopolitan*, May 19, 2017

women as key to peace"[292] in a UN address. And of course there are spiritual leaders like the Dalai Lama who recurrently encourage us to "break the cycle of hatred" by expressing "warmheartedness, kindness and generosity, even in disagreement" with others who "show you contempt or hatred.[293] These perspectives are important. But is it enough?

HOW TECH HAS WORSENED OUR GLOBAL IDENTITY CRISIS

Global values may still be spreading thanks to a greater role played by other actors. But the growing challenge to such values cannot be denied, as xenophobia has deepened. One factor that has allowed this to happen is of course tech. It has exacerbated our global identity crisis, as social media has been dangerously leveraged to instigate xenophobia.

---

[292] Angelina Jolie: Equality for Women Key to Peaceful World, *Washington Post*, Mar 29, 2019

[293] The Dalai Lama and Arthur C. Brooks, The Dalai Lama and Arthur Brooks, All of Us Can Break the Cycle of Hatred, *Washington Post*, Mar 11, 2019

Here are a few examples to consider: UN human rights experts confirmed that Facebook has been used to spread hate speech in Myanmar, turning into a "beast"[294] against local Muslim minorities some are calling a "genocide"[295] (in fact, some anti-Muslim posts have even been reportedly been tied to senior military[296] personnel). In Sri Lanka, Buddhist mobs' anti-Muslim riots[297] have been in part driven by disturbing Facebook posts[298] like "Kill all Muslims, don't let even one child of the dogs escape."[299]

---

[294] Reuters, Facebook: UN Blames Social Media Giant for Spreading Hatred of Rohingya in Myanmar, *ABC Net,* Mar 12, 2018

[295] Krishnadev Calamur, The World Isn't Prepared to Deal With Possible Genocide In Myanmar, *The Atlantic*, Aug 28, 2018

[296] Paul Mozur, A Genocide Incited on Facebook, With Posts From Myanmar's Military, *New York Times*, Oct 15, 2018

[297] Sudha Ramachandran, Sri Lanka's Anti-Muslim Violence, *Diplomat,* Mar 13, 2018

[298] Michael Safi, Sri Lanka Accuses Facebook Over Hate Speech After Deadly Riots, *Guardian*, Mar 14, 2018

[299] Tribune News Service, 'Kill All Muslims, Don't Let Even One Child of the Dogs Escape': In Sri Lanka, Facebook Struggles to Curb Hate Speech, *South China Morning* Post, Apr 1, 2018

In India, both Facebook and WhatsApp messages have promoted fake news and hate speech[300] which led to the killings[301] of certain minorities. In the US and the EU[302], far right extremists have leveraged social media to spread their anti-minority views and violence widely, just as Islamist extremist groups[303] spread their hate.[304] And of course, most recently in March, the mosque shootings[305] in New Zealand[306] by a "white nationalist"[307] were

---

[300] India Hit List of Hindu Muslim Couples Taken Off Facebook, *BBC*, Feb 5, 2018

[301] Matthew Ingram, India Tells WhatsApp to Stop the Deadly Rumor Mill, Somehow, *Columbia Journalism Review*, July 5, 2018

[302] Tom Batchelor, Neo-Nazis Benefiting From Dramatic Rise in Racist Websites to Spread Hate and Incite Violence, UN Warns, *Independent*, Nov 1, 2018

[303] Julia Ebner, *The Rage: The Vicious Circle of Islamist and Far-Right Extremism*, IB Tauris, 2017

[304] Sean Illing, Reciprocal Rage: Why Islamist Extremists and the Far Right Need Each Other, *Vox*, Dec 26, 2018

[305] Jane Coaston, The New Zealand Shooter's Manifesto Shows How White Nationalist Rhetoric Spreads, *Vox*, Mar 18, 2019

[306] Billy Perrigo, The New Zealand Attack Exposed How White Supremacy Has Long Flourished Online, *Time*, Mar 20, 2019

[307] Why White Nationalist Terrorism Is a Global Threat, *Economist*, Mar 21, 2019

streamed live[308] on Facebook[309] – a sad reminder that tech has empowered *all* types of extremist violence globally.[310]

Yes, we all know the regulation of social media, and the tech giants who created it, is key, but we've been debating that for awhile. Facebook and others have also been saying for years that they're doing everything they can to prevent the spread of hate speech through their tech. I've directly heard members of these companies making such public declarations at various conferences, from the NY Times Democracy Forum in Athens, Greece to an online radicalization conference at George Washington University. Ok, great – please keep trying, tech firms.

What *else* can we do?

We clearly need other approaches too. It is encouraging that this year, on the 30-year anniversary of the Internet, its founder Sir

---

[308] Tess Owen, Decoding the Racist Memes the Alleged New Zealand Shooter Used to Communicate, *Vice*, Mar 15, 2019

[309] Sherisse Pham, Facebook, YouTube and Twitter Struggle to Deal with New Zealand Shooting Video, *CNN*, Mar 15, 2019

[310] Charlie Campbell, The New Zealand Attacks Show How White Supremacy Went From a Homegrown Issue to a Global Threat, *Time*, Mar 21, 2019

Tim Berners-Lee recognizes the web "needs more love" and is launching a "fight" against hate.[311] This is a step in the right direction. Developing the counter-narrative to extremism and hate is important. Determining what values are important to us is crucial. Today's global crisis of legitimacy can in fact be a gift to redefine *who* we are.

TECH CURES: CROWDSOURCING NEW GLOBAL VALUES AND USING VIRTUAL REALITY TO EASE OUR GLOBAL IDENTITY CRISIS

There is a larger role for certain state and non-state actors to play in easing this crisis of identity that makes up part of our global legitimacy crisis. Tech is one tool that can be leveraged to understand what our new shared global values might be today. Looking at events of recent years, there are certain values that stand out. Simply consider what citizens have been fighting for around the world, beyond democracy and human rights.

---

[311] Web Needs More Love, Says Its Creator, *BBC,* Nov 2, 2018

A growing tech-driven citizen movement against political corruption in many countries – including South Korea[312], Brazil[313], Slovakia[314] and even Russia[315] – would suggest anti-corruption is an important shared global value. In parts of the EU, including the UK[316], Spain and Greece[317], but also in countries in other regions, like Egypt[318], Sudan[319] and even Iraq[320], it is clear that citizens' major concerns are economic. They require a certain level of subsistence and austerity policies are pushing them below this basic minimum.

[312] James Griffiths, The Sprawling Corruption Scandal That Rocked South Korea, *CNN*, Aug 25, 2017

[313] Dom Phillips, Brazil's Right on the Rise As Anger Grows Over Scandal and Corruption, *Guardian*, July 26, 2017

[314] Thousands Turn Out for Anti-Corruption Protest in Slovakia, *DW*, June 6, 2017

[315] Elizabeth Roberts, Russia's Anti-Corruption Protests Explained, *CNN*, June 12, 2017

[316] Thousands March on Parliament in Anti-Government Protest, *BBC*, July 1, 2017

[317] Protests Erupt in Greece for Second Day Ahead of Major Austerity Vote, *CBS News*, May 18, 2017

[318] Riot Police Fill Streets As Egypt Braces for Austerity Protests, *Enca*, Nov 11, 2016

[319] Kaamil Ahmed, Eight Sudanese Protesters Killed As Anger Rises Over High Living Costs, *Middle East Eye*, Dec 20, 2018

[320] Jennifer Williams, The Violent Protests in Iraq Explained, *Vox*, Sept 8, 2018

Mere economic survival is in this sense a global value, as is internet freedom[321], with citizens protesting in places like Russia[322], Venezuela[323] and parts of Africa.[324] Anti-extremism protests have also recurred in countries across[325] Europe[326] and South Asia.[327] 2019 has also seen the emergence of a powerful youth-led movement[328] in the EU to pressure governments to tackle climate change. Inspired by Swedish teen activist (and

---

[321] Freedom on the Net, *Freedom House*, 2018

[322] Thousands Protests Against Internet Restriction, *Reuters*, Mar 10, 2019

[323] Javier Pallero, Civil Society Unites Against Internet Censorship in Venezuela, *Access Now*, June 1, 2017

[324] Hilary Matfess and Jeffrey Smith, Africa's Attack on Internet Freedom, *Newsweek*, July 23, 2018

[325] Muslim Peace March: Hundreds Take to Cologne Streets to Protest Islamist Terrorism, *Independent*, June 18, 2017

[326] Muslims in Europe Rally Against Extremist Violence, *CBS News*, Sept 26, 2014

[327] 'Death to Daesh!' Thousands Protest Against ISIS in Western Afghanistan, *RT*, Jan 4, 2017

[328] Luisa Beck, 'We Don't Have Time Anymore': In Face of Climate Change, Young People Across Europe Are Protesting For Their Future, *Washington Post*, Feb 15, 2019

Nobel Peace Prize nominee) Greta Thunberg[329], the movement has since spread globally.[330]

So anti-corruption, anti-austerity, pro-internet freedom, anti-extremism and climate change are a few new global values that have emerged. What else do we care about and who will decide it?

Well, governments in theory could try to guide us towards global values and what are global identity is. Then again, they are also confused about what's coming and many citizens struggle to believe in their leaders today. So what will likely be key is to define who we are, separate from government's vision. Maybe now, more than ever, we need new role models to guide us along? There needs to be a clear public message about the very particular identity crisis of today's post-hegemonic world and how we might tackle it.

---

[329] Leslie Hook, The Climate Activist on Becoming the Face of a Global Movement – And Why She Sees Her Asperger's As a Gift, *Financial Times*, Feb 22, 2019

[330] Jessica Glenza, Alan Evans, Hannah Ellis-Petersen and Naaman Zhou, Climate Strikes Held Around the World, *Guardian*, Mar 15, 2019

It doesn't hurt that public figures like the UN Secretary General Antonio Guterres[331] and Pope Francis[332] condemn xenophobia. Former President Obama spoke powerfully after the New Zealand attacks, saying "we must stand against hatred in all its forms."[333] New Zealand Prime Minister Jacinda Ardern has also called for a global fight against racism[334] and let's hope other leaders will join her campaign (frankly if she can lead this important global campaign and create a powerful counter-narrative to hate, she deserves a Nobel Peace Prize nod). But what else?

We must be creative. Tech has already been used as a tool to counter hate and extremist thinking – consider EndX.org, a new online movement to "recapture America's core values of inclusivity, tolerance, pluralism and a firm belief that everyone

---

[331] Eric Walsh, U.N. Chief Guterres Condemns Racism, Xenophobia: Twitter Post, *US News*, Aug 15, 2017

[332] Philip Pullella, Pope Francis Denounces 'Epidemic Of Animosity' Toward Minorities, *Huffington Post*, Nov 19, 2016

[333] Rebecca Morin, Obama on New Zealand Massacre, *Politico*, Mar 15, 2019

[334] Christchurch Shootings: Jacinda Ardern Calls for Global Anti-Racism Fight, *BBC*, Mar 20, 2019

belongs."[335] But perhaps we could do more, like *crowdsource* a new global identity? Let's ask everyone, especially the young, *who* we should be in today's post-hegemonic world. What values should guide us? This question should be crowdsourced from students at high schools and students groups (e.g. Model UN) worldwide. Again, to redefine our identity, we need to create the counter-narrative to extremism[336] and hate. For now, governments don't have the capacity to tackle it – we can as tech-armed citizens, at least we can try.

VR may be another tool of tech to ease this global identity crisis by creating more empathy. Billions of dollars have been invested in VR in recent years for new types of immersive entertainment. It is also being used as a tool to treat social anxiety[337] and post-traumatic stress disorder, especially amongst

[335] EndX.org

[336] Maha Hosain Aziz, Three Steps to Reduce ISIS Recruitment in Western Countries, *Huffington Post*, May 5, 2015

[337] Maria Temming, Using Virtual Reality to Treat Social Anxiety, Post-Traumatic Stress Disorders, *Genetic Literacy Project*, Nov 8, 2018

youth[338] and soldiers.[339] And it has reduced ignorance by allowing viewers to *feel* what life is like as a Rohingya[340] or Syrian refugee.[341]

But could it also make us *less* xenophobic? Research suggests VR has promoted racial[342] sensitivity[343] and greater empathy for those with disabilities, respect for the environment as well as altruism. What if VR was used to challenge the views of the xenophobic citizen (or politician) who doesn't want more refugees in his country or the extremist views of a hate group member?

[338] Kendall Teare, New Yale Lab Will Use Virtual Reality Games to Reduce Risks in Teens, *Yale News*, Nov 15, 2017

[339] Simon Parkin, How Virtual Reality Is Helping Heal Soldiers With PTSD, *NBC News*, Mar 16, 2017

[340] Kyle Melnick, Al Jazeera Releases VR Documentary 'I Am Rohingya", *VR Scout*, Oct 1, 2017

[341] Christopher Malmo, A New Virtual Reality Tool Brings the Daily Trauma of the Syrian War to Life, *Motherboard*, Aug 23, 2014

[342] Melissa Hogenboom, Can Virtual Reality Be Used to Tackle Racism?, *BBC*, Nov 28, 2013

[343] Racial Bias Can Be Reduced Through Virtual Reality, European Researchers Say, *University Herald*, Nov 28, 2013

Yes, this is all idealistic[344] and hypothetical (e.g. *who* would implement this and *how* would we get the xenophobic to participate?), but it's a start. Until we can definitively answer the global identity question, the identity fissures in society will deepen, while hate groups thrive and the minority suffers. If we have starting using tech like blockchain[345] to empower refugees with a digital identity and AI to give them free legal advice[346] via a "robot lawyer"; and leveraged AI to tackle the UN's sustainable development goals[347] and aid in disaster relief efforts[348], why can't we use tech[349] to tackle our global identity crisis? This is the time to be creative. Using tools like tech, we can try to boost empathy to

---

[344] Paul Bloom, It's Ridiculous to Use Virtual Reality to Empathize With Refugees, *The Atlantic*, Feb 3, 2017

[345] Roger Huang, How Blockchain Can Help With The Refugee Crisis, *Forbes*, Jan 27, 2019

[346] Didem Tali, Four AI-Powered Technologies Aimed at Helping Refugees, Dell Technologies, Dell Technologies, Aug 14, 2018

[347] Michael Chui, Rita Chung, Ashley van Heteren, Using AI to Help Achieve Sustainable Development Goals, UNDP, Jan 21, 2019

[348] Christopher Flavelle, AI Startups Promise to Help Disaster Relief and Evacuation, *Bloomberg Businessweek*, Aug 16, 2018

[349] Michael Chui, Martin Harryson, James Manyika, Roger Roberts, Rita Chung, Ashley van Heteren, Pieter Nel, Notes from the AI Frontier Applying AI for Social Good, Discussion Paper, *McKinsey Global Institute*, Dec 2018

counter xenophobia and reclaim positive global values on a mass

scale.

And what you about you, Reader, you tell me:

Are you a globalist or a nationalist – do you care about the

"other" within your borders or elsewhere?

CHAPTER 6

REFLECTING ON OUR UNIQUE GLOBAL LEGITIMACY CRISIS

THE DAWN OF A NEW, GLOBAL AND TECH-DRIVEN ENLIGHTENMENT?

So, Reader, how are you feeling at this point? What do you think about the world today after the past few chapters? *Are you okay?* I know. It's a lot to take in. But I hope each chapter has given you some sense of clarity or even appreciation for what we are facing now: an unprecedented global legitimacy crisis. It should be clear that this really *is* a sensitive turning point for all of us, geopolitically, politically, economically and socially, no matter where we are in the world. Each risk really feeds into the other. And the game changer for our future will be whether we – both governments and citizens – learn to leverage tech as a tool to ease this crisis in the coming years. In fact, it must be a three-way conversation between governments, citizens and of course the techies.

If we take a minute to reflect further on our global legitimacy crisis today, we may also realize how in some ways this may be history repeating itself. In a sense, our situation today resembles the European Enlightenment of the 17th and 18th centuries. Back then, there was a notable challenge to the status quo. A group of scientists, philosophers and writers began questioning traditional ideas in science, religion, philosophy and government – this was partly a response to scientific discovery, the religious Thirty Years War and exposure to other cultures through greater exploration.

These intellectuals spread their criticisms through salons and pamphlets. And of course there were landmark publications like the massive *Encyclopédie*[350] with its 17 volumes of text and 11 volumes of illustrations to educate the average person and more importantly challenge key ideas of religion and the state itself. But this critical period and its publications inspired new ideas, movements and even revolutions in Europe and the US.

Today, we are also faced with a challenge to the status quo.

---

[350] Denis Diderot and Jean Le Rond d'Alembert (editors), *Encyclopédie: Ou Dictionnaire Raisonnée Des Sciences, Des Arts, et Des Métier*, 1772

Every day, we are witnessing distinct trends manifesting themselves in all parts of the world and curiously all at once. And it is leading to new ideas, movements and revolutions. In some ways, it feels like our global legitimacy crisis could be the dawn of a new type of Enlightenment[351] reflective of the 21st century, one which is clearly global and in a sense driven by tech, or at least shaped by it. Let's explore this idea a bit more.

First, like in the original Enlightenment, there is a clear *challenge to the status quo* today – but it is of course happening globally, not just in Europe and the US. Again, we are at a crossroads in four significant areas. Norms have been challenged. What will come next? In many ways, the "future is up for grabs"[352] and it is unclear who is capable or ready to grab it for the greater good.

Geopolitically, the US-led world order of the past few decades seems to be giving way to something new. Maybe it is

---

[351] Maha Hosain Aziz, #1 Has a New, Global and Tech-Driven Enlightenment Begun? *Medium*, June 26, 2018

[352] Gideon Rose, Who Will Run the World? *Foreign Affairs*, Jan/Feb 2019

simply post-hegemonic or perhaps it is officially multipolar? It's still unclear how the world order will evolve but the change in status quo cannot be denied. Politically, tech-armed citizens have been challenging their political systems, in many democracies and dictatorships in notable ways for a while, even bringing down governments or certain political leaders. Is democracy still the best political system? It's just not so clear cut anymore.

Economically, decades of globalization are clashing with growing economic nationalism – similar to what happened in the years leading up to the First World War[353]. At the same time, anxiety also builds about how automation may leave many jobless. Socially, years of dominant global values like democracy and human rights are being overtly challenged by rising autocrats, xenophobia and various strands of extremism in most parts of the world.

Second, like in the past western Enlightenment, there are *a few triggers* that contributed to today's challenge to the status quo.

---

[353] Ana Swanson, The World Today Looks A Bit Like It Did Before World War I But What Does That Mean?, *World Economic Forum*, 2017

At different points in this book, I've alluded to different factors that have gotten us to where we are today. No *one* factor has led us here.

One contributing factor is the 2008 global economic crisis which governments have never fully recovered from. This explains some of the recurring citizen frustration over economic issues which bubble up into protests. Another factor is extremism which has deeply embedded itself in most countries' DNA. It has found a space to flourish and evolve into new variations, no matter what policymakers do. It has created an alternative to values of liberalism and inclusivity which the US-led world order once preached.

But *tech* itself could also be seen as a contributing factor that has certainly shaped our global legitimacy crisis. It is tech that is already changing the very nature of power – the tech cold war has begun and it is tech on the battlefield that likely will determine the next leading superpower of the international system. It is tech that has allowed for the average citizen to be more activist against government, even bringing down entire governments and regimes. It is tech that is changing our economies and our future employment which will wipe out some jobs, even if new ones are created. And it is tech that has facilitated the dramatic spread of xenophobic and extremist ideology that feeds into our global identity crisis.

Finally, like in the original Enlightenment, *new ideas* are spreading and in some cases spurring entire movements; and of course *public intellectuals* are also spreading new ideas to challenge or even replace old paradigms. Today it is happening globally and the very nature of the public intellectual has evolved. New ideas can be spread faster and more widely, thanks of course to tech.

But let's be clear on what we mean by a public intellectual. Historically, the public intellectual was male and a philosopher or some kind of academic. He was known for sharing his critical thinking about society and would offer his solutions for policy problems – especially at times when we were notably divided[354] (e.g. Vietnam war).

Today, we don't see too many fitting that mould, except maybe Bremmer, Khanna, Chomsky and Zakaria, who still try to help the public make sense of the world through their speeches, articles and books that are widely distributed online (side note to you, Reader: where are the *female* public intellectuals? Or maybe I'm simply not aware of them?) We do see more thought leaders[355] – those with one specific idea or expertise which they share widely. But our 21st century, tech-driven and global Enlightenment has its own type of public intellectual spreading his ideas – the activist *tech* billionaire. I know, some of you are already rolling your eyes at the idea of this, because of the recurrent Facebook backlash… Just hang on. Let's take a second to think this through.

---

[354] Elizabeth Mitchell, What Happened to America's Public Intellectuals?, *Smithsonian*, July 2017

[355] David Sessions, The Rise of the Thought Leader: How the Superrich Have Funded a New Class of Intellectual, *New Republic*, June 28, 2017

A ROLE FOR THE ACTIVIST *TECH* BILLIONAIRE

Today there are more billionaires globally than ever before.[356] Yes, these days the very rich elite of the world are facing a "fatcat backlash", as one journalist put it[357] after the 2019 World Economic Forum in Davos. A new book by former *New York Times* columnist Anand Giridharadas[358] aggressively argues the elite who want to change the world are actually making the rest of us worse off. Point taken. Meanwhile, long-time philanthropists, like George Soros for instance, have their fair share of critics (as the *Financial Times'* Gideon Rachman put it, "Soros hatred is a global sickness" for a "new generation of nationalists."[359]) But we cannot deny the role of some activist billionaires, particularly the ones in tech, in actually trying to help us tackle certain global risks today. In many

---

[356] Amanda L. Gordon, <u>The Identity Crisis of the Ultra-Rich: There have never been more billionaires. So what does it mean to be one?</u> *Bloomberg*, Feb 8, 2019

[357] Lionel Laurent, <u>Make No Mistake, Davos, the Fat Cat Backlash Is Coming</u>, *Bloomberg*, Jan 21, 2019

[358] Anand Giridharadas, *Winner Takes All: The Elite Charade of Changing the World*, Alfred A. Knopf, 2018

[359] Gideon Rachman, <u>Soros Hatred Is a Global Sickness</u>, *Financial Times*, Sept 18, 2017

ways, they are a new type of political influencer in our international system – one that we may not want to turn away in light of recurring legitimacy crises of governments.

The activist tech billionaire has become more public in challenging policy and, again for better or worse, is also trying to shape it directly. He sees the writing on the wall in terms of tech's dramatic impact on all aspects of our lives. He is warning us. He is trying to prepare us for this growing impact. In this way, perhaps activist tech billionaires *are* the new public intellectuals of our current and future world order? At this stage, he still has the legitimacy to enlighten us, especially in a world where most political leaders are facing chronic legitimacy crises.

Today, the activist tech billionaire is commenting on major political issues; he is spotting current and future trends, even offering policy proposals to the public. For instance, activist billionaires (and other CEOs) have spoken out about climate change, specifically President Trump's decision to withdraw[360]

----

[360] Kevin Liptak, WH: US Staying Out of Climate Accord, *CNN*, Sept 17, 2017

from the Paris Accords back in 2017. Twitter and Square's Jack Dorsey tweeted how it was "an incredibly shortsighted and backwards move."[361] Dorsey also tweeted against President Trump's ban on the transgender military ban, saying "Discrimination in any form is wrong for all of us"[362], as did many others.

But more often, the activist tech billionaire is warning us about the negative impact of broader trends, for example how tech will impact our economy and society, especially automation-related unemployment. As tech billionaire Ma put it, "in the coming 30 years, the world's pain will be much more than happiness."[363] This has sparked a recurring policy debate among activist billionaires about how UBI might help us cope with tech-related unemployment in the coming years. Slack's Stewart Butterfield suggests "giving people even a very small safety net

---

[361] Kate Vinton, Zuckerberg, Benioff and Other Billionnaires Sound Off on Trump's Decision on Paris Climate Accord, *Forbes*, June 2, 2017

[362] Catherine Clifford, Tech Titans Mark Zuckerberg, Tim Cook, Jack Dorsey Oppose Trump's Ban on Transgender Troops, *CNBC*, July 26, 2017

[363] Arjun Kharpal, Billionaire Jack Ma says CEOs could be robots in 30 years, warns of decades of 'pain' from A.I., internet impact, *CNBC*, April 24, 2017

would unlock a huge amount of entrepreneurialism."[364] Virgin's Richard Branson takes the policy suggestion one step further – AI will wipe out jobs but will create extreme wealth that can be reinvested in part in UBI[365]. Tesla's Elon Musk predicts UBI will be "necessary over time if artificial intelligence takes over most human jobs."[366]

Some activist billionaires are often putting their money where their mouth is. Yes, we've seen this for awhile – think of Soros and his democracy-focused Open Society Foundation or Bill Gates' inequity-focused foundation (and yes, they both have their critics[367]). But in the last few years, we have witnessed a new wave of tech billionaires becoming more aggressively activist in influencing policy. In UBI, Y Combinator's Sam Altman launched

---

[364] Becky Peterson, It's Not Just Zuckerberg – Slack CEO Stewart Butterfield is a Big Fan of Universal Basic Income, *Business Insider*, Aug 4, 2017

[365] Catherine Clifford, Billionaire Richard Branson: Extreme Wealth Generated By AI Industry Should Be Used for Cash Handouts, *CNBC*, Oct 10, 2017

[366] Catherine Clifford, Elon Musk: Free Cash Handouts "Will Be Necessary" If Robots Take Humans' Jobs, *CNBC*, June 18, 2018

[367] Sandi Doughton, New Report Says Gates Foundation Favors Businesses Not Poor, *Seattle Times*, Jan 20, 2016

a small pilot project[368] in Oakland, California, in 2016; now he plans to expand[369] it to be the nation's largest UBI trial[370] and with significant political[371] support. According to his team's blog, their next experiment[372] is to see if people's motivation to work and quality of life improves with UBI.

In climate change, Michael Bloomberg pledged $15 million of his own money[373] to the UN and has also facilitated[374] "a new coalition of cities, businesses and universities" to take a lead role in fighting this global challenge; he also announced he would not run in the 2020 US presidential election as he can create more positive social change as a "private citizen", especially his new

[368] Kia Kokalitcheva, Y Combinator Wants to Test a Revolutionary Economic Idea, *Fortune*, May 31, 2016

[369] Y Combinator Research, Basic Income Project Proposal, Overview for Comments and Feedback, Sept 2017

[370] Kathleen Pender, Oakland Group Plans to Launch Nation's Biggest Basic-Income Research Project, *San Francisco Chronicle*, Sept 21, 2017

[371] California Democratic Party, 2018 Platform, Feb 15, 2018

[372] Chris Weller, One of the Biggest VCs in Silicon Valley Is Launching An Experiment That Will Give 3,000 People Free Money Until 2022, *Business Insider*, Sept 21, 2017

[373] Kristine Phillips, Michael Bloomberg Pledges His Own Money to Help UN After Trump Pulls Out of Paris Climate Deal, *Washington Post*, June 3, 2017

[374] Michael Bloomberg, Trump Won't Stop Americans Hitting the Paris Climate Targets. Here's How We Do It?, *Guardian*, Aug 11, 2017

project Beyond Carbon (a "grassroots effort to begin moving America as quickly as possible away from oil and gas and toward a 100 percent clean energy economy."[375] Other billionaires, led by Gates, have put their funds into a $1 billion venture fund[376] for clean energy tech to fight climate change. And after Hurricane Maria damage (and President Trump's tweets that aid cannot continue "forever"[377]), Tesla's Elon Musk offered to rebuild[378] Puerto Rico's energy infrastructure; 11,000 energy projects[379] are currently in effect.[380]

Clearly, today's public intellectual – the activist tech billionaire – not only helps explain the challenges in status quo to

---

[375] Michael Bloomberg, Our Highest Office, My Deepest Obligation: I'm Not Running for President, But I Am Launching a New Campaign: Beyond Carbon, *Bloomberg*, Mar 5, 2019

[376] Hayley Miller, Bill Gates and Billionaire Buddies Invest $1 Billion In Clean Energy Fund to Fight Climate Change, *Huffington Post*, Dec 13, 2016

[377] Daniella Diaz, Trump: We Cannot Aid Puerto Rico "Forever", *CNN*, Oct 12, 2017

[378] Jake Novak, Elon Musk's Offer to Rebuild Puerto Rico's Electricity Grid is Game Changer, *CNBC*, Oct 9, 2017

[379] Mike Brown, Elon Musk Reveals the Staggering Scale of Tesla's Puerto Rico Solar Projects, *Inverse*, June 4, 2018

[380] Fred Lambert, Tesla Powerwalls and Powerpacks keep the lights on at 662 locations in Puerto Rico during island-wide blackout, says Elon Musk, *Electrek*, Apr 18, 2018

the public, he is also aggressively suggesting and testing new ideas to tackle these challenges. He is trying to ease the global legitimacy crisis, in a sense. At least for now, they are not the techno-elites who turn their back on humanity, as Harari predicts. (A note to you Reader: why are these activist tech billionaires so far largely male – why is that? Where are the women? This *must* change[381] in the future.)

So, move over a little, Chomsky, Bremmer, Khanna and Zakaria – a new category of public intellectual has emerged – the activist tech billionaire who not only shares his views on major issues with the masses, but is also aggressively trying to shape policy. He is filling a void perhaps as politicians muddle through to combat major risks in today's global legitimacy crisis. It's not easy. (Again, Reader, I ask you: where are the female public intellectuals to help make sense of how things are changing? Where are the social scientists? There is definitely room for more voices as we navigate today's unique, tech-influenced global legitimacy crisis.)

---

[381] Financial Times, Robot-Proof Skills That Give Women an Edge in the Age of AI, *Medium*, Feb 12, 2019

A NEW SOCIAL CONTRACT
BETWEEN TECH FIRMS *AND* CITIZENS

Besides a role for the activist tech billionaire, the citizen cannot be ignored in tackling today's global legitimacy crisis. This is a period of declining legitimacy for political leaders and their institutions globally. In some ways, tech firms may have more sway over our lives than our own governments – at least that's how it can feel at times. It may be worthwhile to consider a defined set of guidelines for our relationship with tech. In fact, this may be critical for securing a more secure future world order.

As explained in Chapter Three on the political aspect of our global legitimacy crisis, the social contract[382] is broken globally – at least the one between government and citizens in many democracies and nondemocracies. The recurring citizen protests against political leaders in recent years pretty much everywhere are proof that citizens' expectations of their governments have often

---

[382] Dr Maha Hosain Aziz and Brynnan Parish, Let's Create a Social Contract Between Tech Companies and Citizens, *Huffington Post*, Nov 21, 2017

not been met. Maybe this critical relationship will improve by 2020? Or 2025? Let's see. But as we wait for governments to regain some legitimacy in the eyes of their jaded citizenry, it may be time to consider another critical relationship – the one developing between tech companies and citizens.

Technology is shaping[383] our lives[384] politically, economically and socially every day in positive and negative ways[385], perhaps having a more immediate impact on us than weak governments; this is after all the Fourth Industrial Revolution[386] as the World Economic Forum's Schwab termed it, which will likely only deepen in the coming years. We need to create a new type of social contract – not necessarily between government and citizens, but between tech companies and citizens. A role for tech

383 Fulvia Montresor, The Seven Technologies Changing Your World, World Economic Forum, Jan 19, 2016

384 Josh Lowe, How the iPhone Changed Our Lives, *Newsweek*, Sept 12, 2017

385 David Streitfeld, Tech Giants, Once Seen As Saviors, Are Now Viewed As Threats, *New York Times*, Oct 12, 2017

386 Klaus Schwab, The Fourth Industrial Revolution: What It Means, How To Respond, *World Economic Forum*, Jan 14, 2016

researchers (e.g. New York's Data & Society or London's Dot Everyone[387]) and tech ethicists in defining this contract is key too.

First, we know tech companies are notably impacting our politics, at times creating political change. Social media has allowed for the average citizen to be more activist against government, even bringing down entire governments and regimes. Tech leaders are also speaking out about policy issues like climate change and even trying to shape policy. But we do have to remind ourselves these tech leaders are not elected and cannot be held accountable if their words or actions don't deliver the desired result. Plus, we cannot deny tech's role in politics isn't always positive – there was after all some form of Russian interference[388] online in the US election. A social contract would help us know what to expect of technology's political role, or at least set some guidelines for the positive role it can play.

---

[387] Data & Society is a research institute focused on the "social and cultural issues arising from data-centric technological development". Dot Everyone is a think tank that "champions responsible technology for a fairer future".

[388] Elizabeth Dwoskin and Adam Entous, Google Says Russia Tried to Influence US Election Using Adverts on YouTube and Gmail, *Independent*, Oct 9, 2017

Second, we know tech companies are changing our economies. Yes, some jobs are being wiped out due to automation but new jobs will also be created. Plus tech billionaires are debating UBI for those displaced, testing UBI's viability and suggesting how the funds might come from AI-created wealth. Then again, not everyone will necessarily be open to these new jobs or have access to UBI, potentially becoming precariats with no real "occupational identity", as I explained earlier. We also know that tech can also be leveraged to launch global cyber attacks – apparently "billions" of people were affected by data breaches and cyberattacks in 2018, according to one report from Positive Technologies[389]. One study suggests a major global cyber attack could cause $120 billion in economic damage[390]. A social contract might clarify what we as citizens should expect of technology's impact on our economy – or rather what we *demand*.

[389] Mike Snider, Your Data Was Probably Stolen in Cyberattack in 2018 and You Should Care, *USA Today*, Jan 1, 2019

[390] Tim Worstall, Lloyd's – Extreme Cyberattack Could Cost $120 Billion, As Much As 0.2% Of Global GDP, *Forbes*, July 17, 2017

Third, tech companies are part of our daily social lives. It is how we connect with families and friends globally and learn about the world to make ourselves so we are more informed (at least this was before the dawn of fake news). Social media has become a tool in human rights, for instance exposing injustices like sexual harassment[391] in Hollywood, media and politics. But we also know the pitfalls like social media addiction[392] that leads to depression[393] and even suicide[394]. It has led to more hate groups especially a stronger social media presence that has contributed to our growing identity crisis. A social contract might help us understand what role technology should play in society – or more importantly what *we* demand its positive role should be.

---

[391] #MeToo - Sexual Harassment Stories Sweep Social Media After Weinstein Allegations, *Reuters*, Oct 16, 2017

[392] Tom Embury-Dennis, Man Who Invented "Like" Button Deletes Facebook App Over Addiction Fears, *Independent*, Oct 6, 2017

[393] Melissa G. Hunt, Rachel Marx, Courtney Lipson, Jordyn Young, No Moe FOMO: Limiting Social Media Decreases Loneliness and Depression, *Journal of Social & Clinical Psychology*, Vol. 37, No. 10, pg 751-768, Dec 2018

[394] Doug Criss, A Mom Found Videos on YouTube Kids that Gave Children Instructions on Suicide, *CNN*, Feb 25, 2019

Whether we like it or not, tech companies' influence on our lives is growing every day. Governments will keep calling for some kind[395] of[396] regulation[397] (beyond privacy laws like Europe's GDPR), just as certain and commentators will keep calling for more consideration of the ethics[398] of such tech. This is necessary and important. But for the moment, there is still no clarity about what we as citizens really expect from tech companies, despite their notable impact on our lives.

It's a step in the right direction that the man who created the Internet back in 1989, Sir Tim Berners-Lee, has launched a campaign to save the web from "abuse".[399] This new "contract for the web" will ask tech companies to abide by certain principles –

---

[395] What If Large Tech Firms Were Regulated Like Sewage Companies: Being Treated As Utilities Is Big Tech Firm's Biggest Long-Term Threat, *Economist*, Sept 23, 2017

[396] Rob Picheta, Instagram Is Leading Social Media Platform for Child Grooming, *CNN*, Mar 1, 2019

[397] Adam Lashinsky, Data Regulation Is Coming For Big Tech, *Fortune*, Mar 1, 2018

[398] Rachel Coldicutt, The Tech Industry Needs a Moral Compass, *Medium*, Nov 13, 2017

[399] Laurence Dodds, Sir Tim Berners-Lee launches 'Magna Carta for the web' to save internet from abuse, *Telegraph*, Nov 5, 2018

so far apparently Google and Facebook have agreed. Is this enough? Again, it's a step in the right direction. But we can do more. We *must*.

It's time for a group of tech leaders, technologists *and* citizens to get together in a G7-like setting to define this new social contract – that deepening relationship between tech companies and citizens. There is much uncertainty ahead that we may not be fully prepared for, from possible wars to terrorist attacks and more climate change disasters with the backdrop of a global legitimacy crisis, but perhaps with a social contract we can at least try to get a handle on how tech will – or should – shape our lives?

WRAPPING UP MY BOOK

That's it for now, Reader. I hope my particular vision for the world today and in the coming years – a global legitimacy crisis worsened by tech – hasn't depressed you. If you have been feeling anxious about what's happening around you, perhaps I've managed to give you a bit of clarity? But again, you don't have to agree with me. At the very least, I hope the ideas in this book will spark your own discussions about our future world order, wherever in the world you may be reading this from.

What do *you* want our collective future to be? What do your fellow citizens want our future to be?

Above all, please remember that there *is* hope. These risks may be deeply rooted in our existence and yes, it is unlikely that all these crises will suddenly be resolved... But we are *all* in the same boat, facing the *same* challenges in most countries globally. We also each have a role to play in overcoming these challenges.

As we wait for the international system to regain a clear structure; for governments of all types to regain some legitimacy; for globalization to reorient itself; and for a return to some sense of shared global values, what can we do – or rather, what can *you* do, Reader – to help tackle these issues? In this book, I've hinted recurrently that tech, if strategically leveraged, might ease some of these major crises in the interim, as we await the global and national leadership we so crave. But what do *you* think – what should we do?

Think big, think small – either way, please just think.

Yours,

Maha

ABOUT THE AUTHOR

 Dr Maha Hosain Aziz specializes in global risk and prediction. She is a professor in New York University's (NYU) MA International Relations program who also teaches online via Pioneer Academics; a visiting research fellow at the London School of Economics's (LSE) Institute of Global Affairs; and a blogger at *Medium.com*; on occasion, she still consults with governments and corporates via crowdsourced consultancy Wikistrat and other networks. And she is a cartoonist who drew the 2016 political comic book *The Global Kid* (www.theglobalkid.org) for tweens, with all sales going to youth education nonprofits (Pakistan-based Developments in Literacy and US-based Global Glimpse); it won three awards globally (US, Iceland, Pakistan) and is being adapted into a political graphic novel for adults.

Previously, Dr Aziz was a senior fellow at New York think tank World Policy Institute; taught British politics and democratic theory at the LSE and South Asian politics at the School of

Oriental and African Studies (SOAS); wrote a *Bloomberg Businessweek* column on global politics; blogged for the *Huffington Post, CNN's Global Public Square* and the *Observer;* and worked in investment banking at Credit Suisse First Boston.

She is a social scientist who trained at Brown (BA), Columbia (MA) and the LSE (MSc, PhD); she also completed a certification in leveraging the crowd in the public sector at NYU's GovLab. And she is a Jordanian-born Pakistani who grew up in the Middle East (Jordan, Saudi Arabia), Southeast Asia (Singapore, Malaysia), Europe (UK, Greece) and the US.

FUTURE WORLD ORDER (2019) is Dr Aziz's first book. It is for all audiences – from the silent generation to post-millennials – to make better sense of the world at this sensitive turning point. 15% of her book profits are going to her late brother's memorial fund, the *Abid Aziz Fund*, which supports charity Peace & Sport's youth project in Jordan's Za'atari refugee camp. Follow Dr Aziz on <u>LinkedIn</u>, <u>Instagram</u>, <u>Twitter</u> and <u>Facebook</u> and <u>Medium.com</u>.

ABOUT THE ABID AZIZ FUND AT CHARITY PEACE AND SPORT

 Abid Aziz passed away from cancer at age 43 on Dec. 3, 2017, in London. For 18 months, he fought hard, with a smile and now is in a better place. Through out his life, Abid was hopelessly devoted to his family and a caring, sincere friend to many; he only ever wanted to see his loved ones happy. He was highly intelligent and analytical, passionate about his work in the financial markets in New York, Bahrain, Hong Kong and London.

But his lifelong passion was most certainly sports – cricket, tennis, darts, football, you name it. Over the years, he travelled the globe to watch his favorite teams play, from Jamaica to South Africa and Sri Lanka. Most recently in the UK, he frequented cricket tournaments to root for his native Pakistan and football matches to cheer on his beloved Liverpool FC. This was a passion he also shared with his nine year old daughter and his wife.

To commemorate Abid and his incredible love for sports, a memorial tea was held with his friends and family at the home of his beloved cricket, London's historic Lords club; a stone honors him at his favorite Liverpool FC's Anfield Stadium; a memorial fund was also launched at charity Peace and Sport; 15 percent of profits from *FUTURE WORLD ORDER* will be given to the <u>Abid Aziz Fund</u> which supports Peace and Sport's "Live Together" program for Syrian refugee youth in Jordan's Za'atari camp.

Peace and Sport brings together and develops partnerships between the Peace (NGOs, UN Agencies, Academics), the Sport (Olympic Family, International Federations, National Olympic Committees, Athletes) and the Political worlds with the aim of implementing and ensuring the sustainability of field programs, maximizing the use of sport for development and peace and leading social transformation in every area of the world affected by poverty or social instability.

BIBLIOGRAPHY

CHAPTER 1: INTRODUCTION TO OUR
GLOBAL LEGITIMACY CRISIS

Leon Festinger, *Theory of Cognitive Dissonance*, Stanford University Press, 1957

James Kirchick, Blaming Trump for their problems is the one thing Europeans can agree on, *Brookings Institution,* Feb 15, 2019

Graeme Wearden, 'President Trump' as big a threat as jihadi terror to global economy - EIU, *The Guardian,* Mar 17, 2016

Áine Cain, Nine Famous Predictions By Nostradamus Some People Say Foresaw the Future, *Business Insider*, May 14, 2018

Dr Ian Bremmer and Dr Preston Keat, *The Fat Tail: The Power of Political Knowledge in an Uncertain World,* Oxford University Press, 2009

Michele Wucker, *The Gray Rhino*, St Martins Press, 2016

Dr Nassim Taleb, *The Black Swan*, Random House, 2010

Clive Thompson, *New York Times*, Can Game Theory Predict When Iran Will Get the Bomb? Aug 12, 2009

Nate Silver, *The Signal and the Noise, Why So Many Predictions Fail – And Some Don't,* Penguin, 2012

Eric Siegel, *Predictive Analytics: The Power to Predict Who Will Click, Buy, Lie or Die*, Wiley, 2016

Daniel W. Drezner, *The Ideas Industry*, Oxford University Press, 2017

Louis Menand, *New Yorker*, Everybody's An Expert, Dec 5, 2005

Philip Tetlock, *Expert Political Judgement: How Good Is It? How Can We Know?*, Princeton University Press, 2005

Condaleeza Rice and Amy B. Zegart, *Political Risk: How Businesses and Organizations Can Anticipate Global Insecurity*, Twelve Books, 2018

Philip Tetlock and Dan Gardner, *Superforecasting: The Art and Science of Prediction*, Crown Pubishers, 2016

Alix Spiegel, So You Think You're Smarter than a CIA Agent, *NPR*, Apr 2, 2014

David Wallis-Wells' *The Uninhabitable Earth: Life After Warming*, Tim Duggan Books, 2019

Top Risks 2019, Eurasia Group, Jan 7, 2019

Global Risks Report 2019, World Economic Forum, Jan 15, 2019

Maha Hosain Aziz, What Are the Global Risks to Watch in 2019?, *Medium*, Jan 9, 2019

World Economic Outlook Update, IMF, Jan 2019

Kai-Fu Lee, *AI Superpowers: China, Silicon Valley, and the New World Order*, Houghton Mifflin Harcourt, 2018

Yuval Noah Harari, *Homo Deus: A Brief History of Tomorrow*, Harvill Secker, 2016

Kai-Fu Lee, How AI Can Co-Exist with Humans, *Medium*, Oct 18, 2018

John Haltiwanger, New Zealand's Prime Minister Calls For a Global Fight Against Racism and an End to Scapegoating Immigrants After Mass Shooting, *Business Insider*, Mar 20, 2019

Facebook Faces a Reputational Meltdown, *The Economist*, Mar 22, 2018

Mark Sullivan, On CNN, Mark Zuckerberg Scrambles to Rebuild Trust, *Fast Company*, Nov 21, 2018

Steven Pinker, *Enlightenment Now: The Case for Reason, Science, Humanism and Progress*, Viking, 2018

Hans Rosling, *Factfulness: Ten Reasons We're Wrong About the World – and Why Things Are Better Than We Think*, Flatiron Books, 2018

CHAPTER 2: GEOPOLITICAL CRISIS

Christopher Hill, *Changing Politics of Foreign Policy*, Palgrave Macmillan, 2003

Zbigniew Brzezinski, *The Grand Chessboard: American Primacy and Its Geostrategic Imperatives*, Basic Books, 1997

Elke Krahmann, American Hegemony or Global Governance? Competing Visions of International Security, *International Studies Review*, Vol. 7, No. 4, pg 531-545, Dec 2005

Joseph Nye, *Soft Power: The Means to Success in World Politics*, Public Affairs, 2005

Josef Joffe, How America Does It, *Foreign Affairs*, Sept/Oct 1997

Michael Mastanduno & Ethan Kapstein, *Unipolar Politics: Realism and State Strategies After the Cold War*, Columbia University Press, 1999

Charles Krauthmatter, The Unipolar Moment, *Foreign Affairs*, America and the World 1990 Issue

Ian Bremmer, The Era of American Leadership Is Over, *Time*, Dec 19, 2016

Howard Stoffer, What Trump's 'America First' Policy Could Mean for the World, *Time*, Nov 14, 2016

Parag Khanna, Waving Goodbye to US Hegemony, *New York Times Magazine*, Jan 2, 2008

Noam Chomsky, America Is An Empire In Decline, *Salon*, May 10, 2016

Christopher Layne, The Waning of US Hegemony – Myth or Reality? A Review Essay, *International Security*, Vol. 34, No. 1, pg 147-172, Summer, 2009

Remarks by President Trump in Joint Address to Congress, *www.WhiteHouse.Gov*, Feb 28, 2017

Remarks by President Trump to the 72nd Session of the United Nations General Assembly, *www.WhiteHouse.Gov,* Sept 19, 2017

Noam Chomsky, *Hegemony or Survival: America's Quest for Global Dominance*, Penguin, 2004

Michael Shear and Michael Gordon, 63 Hours: From Chemical Attack to Trump's Strike in Syria, *New York Times*, Apr 7, 2017

W. J. Hennigan, Trump Orders Strikes on Syria Over Chemical Weapons, *Time*, Apr 13, 2018

Bianca Britton, 'Pouring Gas On Fire': Russia Slams Trump's Stance in Venezuela, *CNN*, Jan 24, 2019

Stuart Varney interview with John Bolton, *Fox Business*, Jan 24, 2019

'Good for business': Trump adviser Bolton admits US interest in Venezuela's 'oil capabilities', *RT*, Jan 28, 2019

Reid Standish and Emily Tamkin, Europe and US Move to Fight Russian Hybrid Warfare, *Foreign Policy*, Apr 11, 2017

Paul Watson, A Melting Arctic Could Spark a New Cold War, *Time*, May 12, 2017

Greg Wilford, Emmanuel Macron Offers Refuge to American Climate Scientists After Donald Trump Takes US Out of Paris Climate Deal, *Independent*, June 3, 2017

Unresolved: The Techonomic Cold War with China, Intelligence Squared US Debate, Feb 25, 2019

Fareed Zakaria, *Post-American World*, W. W. Norton, 2008

Ian Bremmer and Nouriel Roubini, A G-Zero World: The New Economic Club Will Produce Conflict, Not Cooperation, *Foreign Affairs*, March/ Apr 2011 Issue

Ian Bremmer, *Every Nation for Itself: Winners and Losers in a G-Zero World*, Portfolio, 2012

Kishore Mahbubani, *Has The West Lost It? A Provocation*, Allen Lane, 2018

Parag Khanna, *Future Is Asian: Commerce, Conflict & Culture in the 21st Century*, Simon & Schuster, 2019

Salih Booker and Ari Rickman, The Future Is African – and the United States Is Not Prepared, *Washington Post*, June 6, 2018

John McKenna, Six Numbers that Prove the Future Is African, *World Economic Forum*, May 2, 2017

Bernard-Henri Levy, *Empire and the Five Kings: America's Abdication and the Fate of the World*, Henry Holt & Co, 2019

Moises Naim, *The End of Power: From Boardrooms to Battlefields and Churches to States, Why Being In Charge Isn't What It Used To Be*, Basic Books, 2014

Maha Hosain Aziz with Doreen Horschig, Yu-Ting (Wendy) Sun, Arsh Harjani and Yueyue Jiang, It's a Post-Hegemonic World and That's OK, *Huffington Post*, July 1, 2017

Chris Strohm, US Intelligence Warns That Russia and China Are Seizing on Global Turmoil, *Bloomberg*, Jan 22, 2019

Imogen Foulkes, Why the UN Is Wary of the US Position on Human Rights, *BBC*, May 9, 2017

Suzanne Nossel, It's OK That Trump Doesn't Care about Human Rights, *Foreign Policy*, June 19, 2017

Matt Taibbi, The Anti-Refugee Movement Is America at Its Most Ignorant, *Rolling Stone,* Feb 1, 2017

Nicolas Kristof, Canada, Leading the Free World, *New York Times*, Feb 4, 2017

Rob Gillies, Trudeau says Canada will take refugees banned by US, *PBS*, Jan 28, 2017

Netherlands Government to Counter Trump Abortion Funding Ban, *BBC*, Jan 25, 2017

Dutch Commit $10 Million to Replace Lost US Abortion Funding, *Reuters*, Jan 28, 2017

Jon Sharman, Norway Joins Dutch International Abortion Fund to Combat Donald Trump's Aid Ban, *Independent*, Feb 21, 2017

Daniel Boffey, Mayors of 7,400 Cities Vow to Meet Obama's Climate Commitments, *Guardian*, June 28, 2017

Lizette Alvarez, Mayors, Sidestepping Trump, Vow to Fill Void on Climate Change, *New York Times*, June 26, 2017

Reid Wilson, California Signs Deal with China to Combat Climate Change, *The Hill*, June 6, 2017

Ralph Ellis, Protesters Across Globe Rally for Women's Rights, *CNN*, Jan 22, 2017

Chelsea Bailey and Katie Wong, Global Demonstrations Over Trump's Policies Heat Up Amid Anger Over Travel Ban, *NBC News*, Feb 4, 2017

Helen Davidson and Oliver Milman, Global 'March for Science' Protests Call for Action on Climate Change, *Guardian*, Apr 22, 2017

Christopher Woody, These Are the 25 Most Powerful Militaries in the World – and There's a Clear Winner, *Business Insider*, June 18, 2018

Maha Hosain Aziz, #2 Could a Global AI Treaty Be Key to Future Stability?, *Medium*, June 29, 2018

Greg Allen and Taniel Chan, AI and National Security, Harvard's Belfer Center for Science and International Affairs, 2017

Tom Simonite, AI Could Revolutionize War As Much As Nukes, *Wired*, July 19, 2017

David Meyer, Vladimir Putin Says Whoever Leads in Artificial Intelligence Will Rule the World, Sept 4, 2017

Harold C. Hutchison, Russia Says It Will Ignore Any UN Ban of Killer Robots, Nov 30, 2017

Bill Gertz, AI Weapons: China and America Are Desperate to Dominate This New Technology, *National Interest,* May 30, 2018

Tom O'Connor, Will Robots Fight the Next War? US and Russia Bring Artificial Intelligence to the Battlefield, *Newsweek*, Jan 30, 2018

Matt Stroud, The Pentagon Is Getting Serious About AI Weapons: "We must see to it that we cannot be surprised," says the Pentagon's top scientist, *Verge,* Apr 12, 2018

Jon Christian, Bill Gates Compares Artificial Intelligence to Nuclear Weapons, *Futurism*, Mar 19, 2018

Tom Simonite, For Superpowers, AI Fuels New Global Arms Race, *Wired*, Sept 8, 2017

Anthony Giddens, A Magna Carta for the Digital Age, *Washington Post*, May 2, 2018

Sean Hollister, Google's Project Maven Work Could Have Been Weaponized, Ex-Pentagon Official Admits, *CNET*, June 26, 2018

Paresh Dave, Google Bars Uses of Its Artificial Intelligence Tech in Weapons, *Reuters*, June 7, 2018

Rachel Kraus, The US Army Will Give Startups Who Invent New Weapons a Cash Prize, *Mashable*, June 22, 2018

Amanda Macias, Weapons of the Future: Here's the New War Tech Lockheed Martin Is Pitching to the Pentagon, *CNBC*, Mar 6, 2018

Jon Harper, Pentagon Set to Boost Spending on High-Tech Armaments, *National Defense*, June 27, 2018

James Vincent, Elon Musk and AI Leaders Call for a Ban on Killer Robots: 116 experts in the field have signed a petition as UN talks on the subject are delayed, *Verge*, Aug 21, 2017

Pallab Ghosh, Call to Ban Killer Robots in Wars, *BBC*, Feb 15, 2019

Will Knight, AI Arms Control May Not Be Possible, Warns Henry Kissinger, *MIT Technology Review*, Mar 1, 2019

Brian Wheeler, Terrorists 'Certain' to Get Killer Robots, Says Defence Giant, *BBC*, Nov 30, 2017

Treaty on the Non-Proliferation of Nuclear Weapons (NPT), United Nations

Marc Champion, 'We Have a Real Problem.' U.S. Is at Odds With European Allies, Munich Meeting Shows, *Time*, Feb 17, 2019

David Wemer, Now is the Time to Fight for Freedom, Prosperity, and Peace, Global Democratic Leaders Say, *Atlantic Council Blog*, Feb 24, 2019

CHAPTER 3: POLITICAL CRISIS

Maha Hosain Aziz, The Age of Protests, *CNN*, April 23, 2012

Joanna Jolly, Nepal: Man Who Hit Politician Hailed 'A Hero', *BBC*, Jan 26, 2011

India Agriculture Minister Sharad Pawar Slapped, *BBC*, Nov 24, 2011

Telegraph Video, Protester Slaps Italian Far-Right Politician, *Telegraph*, Nov 9, 2014

Maya Oppenheim, Brazilian Politician Pelted with Eggs By Protesters at Her Own Wedding, *Independent*, July 16, 2017

Telegraph Video, German MP Slapped in the Face with Chocolate Cake Over Stance on Refugees, May 29, 2016

Megan McCluskey, Teen in Viral Video Eggs Australian Politician Who Blamed Immigration for New Zealand Mosque Shootings, *Time*, Mar 16, 2019

Nicholas Vinocur, Emmanuel Macron Pelted with Eggs by Angry Mob, *Politico*, Mar 6, 2016

Lilia Blaise, Self-Immolation, Catalyst of the Arab Spring, Is Now a Grim Trend, *New York Times*, July 9, 2017

Teo Kermeliotis, Austerity Drives Up Suicide Rate in Debt-Ridden Greece, *CNN*, Apr 6, 2012

Clashes in Chile as Thousands of Students Protest Lagging Education Reform, *RT*, Aug 22, 2014

Thousands Rally Against Portuguese Austerity, *Al Jazeera*, Oct 19, 2013

Maha Hosain Aziz, Why Trump's Win Isn't So Shocking: A Six Year Glbal Crisis of Political Legitimacy, *Huffington Post*, Nov 28, 2016

Michael Safi, Have Millennials Given Up On Democracy?, *Guardian*, Mar 18, 2016

Rebecca Burgess, Have Millennials Fallen Out of Love with Democracy? *Newsweek*, Sept 2, 2016

Yascha Mounk and Roberto Stefan Foa, Yes, People Really Are Turning Away From Democracy, *Washington Post*, Dec 8, 2016

Yascha Mounk, *People vs Democracy: Why Our Freedom Is In Danger and How to Save It,* Harvard University Press, 2018

Francis Fukuyama, End of History, *National Interest*, No. 16, pg 3-18, Summer 1989

Ishaan Tharoor, The Man Who Declared the "End of History" Now Fears for Democracy's Future, *Washington Post*, Feb, 9, 2017

Josh Rogin, State Department Considers Scrubbing Democracy Promotion from Its Mission, *Washington Post*, Aug 1, 2017

Jennifer Rubin, Why Editing Out Democracy Matters, *Washington Post*, Aug 1, 2017

Marc Fisher, In Tunisia Act of One Fruit Vendor Sparks Wave of Revolution through the Arab World, *Washington Post*, Mar 26, 2011

Shane Dixon Kavanaugh and Gilad Shiloach, Arab Spring Aftermath: More Conflict, Instability in the Middle East, *Vocativ*, Jan 25, 2016

Maha Hosain Aziz, What Are the Occupiers Really Fighting For? *CNN*, April 18, 2012

Gillian Parker, Nigeria Paralyzed by "Occupy" Protests Over Gas Prices, *Time*, Jan 9, 2012

Chile Protests: Al Jazeera's Faul Lines Follows Student Movement, *Huffington Post*, Jan 4, 2012

Occupy Protest in Manila, Philippines – In Pictures, *Guardian*, Dec 7, 2011

Paul Mason, *Why It's Kicking Off Everywhere: The New Global Revolutions*, Verso Books, 2011

Elinda Labropoulou, Thousands Protest Austerity Measures in Greece, *CNN*, Sept 26, 2012

Raphael Minder, Tens of Thousands Protest Austerity in Spain, *New York Times*, May 13, 2012

Holly Ellyatt and Silvia Amaro, Are We Witnessing the End of Austerity – and What Does That Mean for Europe? *CNBC*, Dec 5, 2018

Phoebe Fronista, For Greece's Austerity-Hit Elderly, Bailout "Will Never End", Aug 17, 2018

Egypt Protests: Mass Celebrations in Cairo As President Morsi Ousted in Coup, *Telegraph*, 2013

Bangkok Tense As 100,000 Protesters Rally Against Yingluck Shinawatra's Adminstration, *ABC*, Nov 24, 2013

What Lies Behind the Protests in Venezuela? *BBC*, March 2, 2014

Pia Riggirozzi, Venezuela Is Putting Democracy and Its Legitimacy to Test, *The Conversation*, Feb 14, 2019

Sam Frizell, Ukraine Protesters Seize Kiev As President Flees, *Time*, Feb 22, 2014

Bruce Douglas, Brazilian President Under Fire As Tens of Thousands Protest in 200 Cities, *Guardian*, Aug 15, 2015

Simon Romero, Dilma Rouseff Is Ousted As Brazil's President in Impeachment Vote, *New York Times*, Aug 31, 2016

Maha Hosain Aziz, British PM Theresa May Faces a Rocky Road Ahead, *Observer*, Aug 2016

South Korea's Presidential Scandal, *BBC*, April 6, 2018

Editorial Board, Malaysia's Arrest of a Corrupt Politician Is a Step Toward Justice, *Washington Post*, July 4, 2018

Vanessa Romo, Former South Korea President Sentenced to 8 More Years in Prison, *NPR*, July 20, 2018

Chile's Students Launch First Protest Under Pinera Adminstration, *Reuters*, Apr 19, 2018

Poland Protests: Thousands Rally Against Court Changes, *BBC*, July 27, 2018

Mohammed Alamin and Mike Cohen, Why Protests Are Raging Against Sudan's Leader, *Washington Post*, Mar 6, 2019

Sudan's President Bashir Steps Down As Ruling Party Leader, *Al Jazeera*, Mar 1, 2019

Algeria's Bouteflika Warns of 'Chaos' Ahead of Protests Against Him, *BBC*, Mar 7, 2019

Benjamin Soloway, Power to the People, *Foreign Policy*, Winter 2019

Merlin Delcid and Jack Guy, The Strange Political Path of Nayib Bukele, El Salvador's New President, *CNN*, Feb 10, 2019

Nontobeko Mlambo, Botswana: Meet Botswana's Youngest Minister, Bogolo Kenewendo, *AllAfrica*, Apr 6, 2018

Maha Hosain Aziz, Democracy or Dictatorship, Does It Even Matter Anymore?, *Huffington Post*, Aug 7, 2017

Emma Luxton, Four Billion People Still Don't Have Internet Access. Here's How to Connect Them, May 11, 2016

UN, The Promotion, Protection and Enjoyment of Human Rights on the Internet, *Human Rights Council*, June 27, 2016

Jessi Hempel, Social Media Made the Arab Spring But Couldn't Save It, *Wired*, Jan 26, 2016

Maeve Shearlaw, Armed with Smartphones And Memes, Zimbabwe's Protesters Find Their Voice Online, July 11, 2016

Bruce Mutsvairo, Can Robert Mugabe Be Tweeted Out of Power?, July 26, 2016

The Man Behind #ThisFlag, Zimbabwe's Accidental Movement For Change, Daily Maverick, May 26, 2016

Sofia Lotto Persio, Contraception in Poland: Government Pushes Ahead with Law Restricting Access to Morning After Pill, *Newsweek*, May 17, 2017

Agnieszka Barteczko and Pawel Florkiewicz, Polish President Halts Justice Reforms After Days of Protests, July 24, 2017

Maha Hosain Aziz, Time for a New Social Contract? *Huffington Post*, Aug 25, 2017

Evelyn Nieves, Fighting for Basic Rights in Morocco, *New York Times*, July 27, 2017

Thousands in Brazil Protest Gutting of Anticorruption Measures, *New York Times*, Apr 12, 2016

Reuters, Spain: Anti-Austerity Protest Attracts Thousands, *Euronews*, Dec 18, 2016

James Edgar, Thousands Gather for Athens Anti-Austerity Protest, *Euronews*, Feb 21, 2017

Eillie Anzilotti, This Plan For An AI-Based Direct Democracy Outsources Votes To A Predictive Algorithm, *Fast Company*, Apr 12, 2018

Yuval Noah Harari, Why Technology Favors Tyranny, *The Atlantic*, Oct 2018

Daniella Cheslow, Zimbabwe Orders Second Internet Shutdown In A Week Of Deadly Protests, *NPR*, Jan 18, 2019

Russia Internet Freedom: Thousands Protest Against Cyber-Security Bill, *BBC*, Mar 10, 2019

Vivian Salama, Trump Tweets Send Advisers Scrambling to Reshape Policy, *Boston Globe*, Aug 3, 2017

We Have Built a Digital Society And So Can You, https://e-estonia.com/

Innar Liiv, Welcome To E-Estonia, The Tiny Nation That's Leading Europe In Digital Innovation, *Huffington Post*, Apr 4, 2017

Utsav Gandhi, This Chicago Startup Is Changing How Governments Interact With Citizens, *Chicago Inno*, July 6, 2017

Embracing Innovation in Government: Global Trends, *OECD*, Feb 2017

César Hidalgo, A Bold Idea to Replace Politicians, TED2018

Jeff John Roberts, Brits Scramble to Google "What is the EU?" Hours After Voting to Leave It, *Fortune*, June 24, 2016

Tanja Aitamurto, Crowdsourcing for Democracy: New Era in Policy-Making, Committee for the Future, *Parliament of Finland*, 2012

Harvey Morris, Crowdsourcing Iceland's Constitution, *New York Times*, Oct 24, 2012

Haroon Siddique, Mob Rule: Iceland Crowdsources Its Next Constitution, *Guardian*, June 9, 2011

Orion Jones, Crowdsourcing Legislation in Finland, *Big Think*, Oct 26, 2012

Tanja Aitamurto, Helene Landemore, David Lee and Ashish Goel, Seven Lessons From the Crowdsourced Law Reform in Finland, *GovLab Blog*, Oct 30, 2013

Maha Hosain Aziz, The Rise of Anti-Government Protests Around the World and How to Reduce It in 2015, *Huffington Post*, Dec 31, 2014

Bruce Bueno de Mesquita and Alastair Smith, *The Dictator's Handbook: Why Bad Behavior Is Almost Always Good Politics*, Public Affairs, 2011

Iain Marlow and Anusha Ondaatjie, Why Sri Lanka Risks Return to Violence, *Washington Post*, Dec 13, 2018

Maha Hosain Aziz, How Crowdsourcing Anti-Corruption Policy Might Ease Brazil's Legitimacy Crisis, *Huffington Post*, Aug 25, 2015

Charles W. Yost, The United Nations: Crisis of Confidence and Will, *Foreign Affairs*, Oct 1966

Séverine Autesserre, The Crisis of Peacekeeping: Why the UN Can't End Wars, *Foreign Affairs*, Jan/Feb 2019

UN Secretary-General's Strategy on New Technologies, Sept 2018

Simeon Tegel, Corruption Scandals Have Ensnared Three Peruvian Presidents: Now the whole political system could change, *Washington Post*, Aug 12, 2018

Iraq's Electricity Minister Fired After Weeks of Protests, *DW*, July 29, 2018

Max Bearak, Kenyans Have Had It with Corruption: Their leaders may finally be doing something about it, *Washington Post*, July 17, 2018

Tatiana Jancarikova, Slovak Protesters Demand More Resignations Over Corruption Neglect, *Reuters*, Apr 15, 2018

Maha Hosain Aziz, #3 Could Blockchain Ease Governments' Chronic Legitimacy Crises? *Medium*, Aug 3, 2018

Promise and Peril: Blockchain, Bitcoin and the Fight Against Corruption, *Transparency International*, Jan 31, 2018

Eduardo Aldaz Carroll, Can Cryptocurrencies and Blockchain Help Fight Corruption?, *World Bank*, Feb 20, 2018

Carlos Santiso, Can Blockchain Help in the Fight Against Corruption?, *World Economic Forum*, Mar 12, 2018

Carlos Santiso, Will Blockchain Disrupt Government Corruption? *Stanford Innovation Social Review*, Mar 5, 2018

Nicky Woolf, What Could Blockchain Do for Politics? *Medium*, Jan 8, 2018

Nick Tsakanikas, Mexico Aims to Eliminate Corruption in Public Tenders Using Blockchain Technology, *BitRates*, Aug 3, 2018

David Floyd, Mexico Tests Blockchain to Track Public Contract Bids, Apr 5, 2018

Sharanya Haridas, This Indian City Is Embracing BlockChain Technology -- Here's Why, *Forbes*, Mar 5, 2018

Kevin Mwanza and Henry Wilkins, African Startups Bet On Blockchain to Tackle Land Fraud, *Reuters*, Feb 16, 2018

Nick Ismail, GovTech to Hit $1 Trillion By 2025, *Information Age*, Nov 12, 2018

CHAPTER 4: ECONOMIC CRISIS

Roubini Warns of 'Perfect Storm' Stalling Global Growth in 2020, *Bloomberg Surveillance TV Show*, Sept 7, 2018

Lori Ioannou, IMF Chair Christine Lagarde Cuts Global Growth Forecast for 2019 to 3.5 Percent, *CNBC*, Jan 22, 2019

Sam Meredith, Trump's Trade War with China Is 'the Biggest Risk to the Global Economy,' BlackRock Exec Says, *CNBC*, Sept 4, 2018

Bloomberg, Jack Ma Says Trade War Is the 'Most Stupid Thing' as U.S.-China Tensions Boil, *Time*, Nov 5, 2018

Ian Bremmer and Cliff Kupchan, Risk 3: Global Tech Cold War, Top Risks for 2018 Report, Eurasia Group, 2018

Eamon Barrett, Ex-Google Exec Kai-Fu Lee Says China Is Winning the Race to Implement AI, Fortune, Nov 29, 2019

Jansen Tham, Why 5G Is the Next Front of US-China Competition, Diplomat, Dec 13, 2018

Kieran O'Hara and Wendy Hall, Four Internets: The Geopolitics of Digital Governance, Centre for International Governance Innovation, CIGI Paper No. 206, Dec 7, 2018

Wendy Hall, The Internet Risks Fracturing Into Quarters, *Financial Times*, Dec 11, 2018

Maha Hosain Aziz, What Are the Global Risks to Watch in 2019?, *Medium*, Jan 9, 2019

Margaret Besheer, ILO Fights Global Youth Unemployment Crisis, *Voice of America*, Feb 2, 2016

World Employment and Social Outlook: Trends 2019, ILO, Feb 13, 2019

Max Ehrenfreund, World Leaders Find Hope for Globalization in Davos Amid Populist Revolt, *Washington Post*, Jan 17, 2017

Martin Crutsinger and Paul Wiseman, Leaders of IMF and World Bank Defend Globalization, *US News*, Apr 20, 2017

A Brief History of the Anti-Globalization Movement, *DW*, June 7, 2017

Noah Smith, The Dark Side of Globalization: Why Seattle's 1999 Protesters Were Right, *The Atlantic*, Jan 6, 2014

Scott Neuman, Anti-Globalization Protests Spark Violence In Hamburg For Second Day, *NPR*, July 7, 2017

Marc Champion, The Rise of Populism, *Bloomberg*, Jan 22, 2019

William A. Galston, Rise of European Populism and the Collapse of the Center-Left, *Brookings Institution*, Mar 8, 2018

Robert Muggah and Brian Winter, Is Populism Making a Comeback in Latin America? *Foreign Policy*, Oct 23, 2017

Ana Swanson, The World Today Looks Ominously Like It Did Before World War I, *Washington Post*, Dec 29, 2016

Maha Hosain Aziz #4 Time to Rebuild Our Moral Economy? Tech May Be Key., *Medium*, Oct 14, 2018

White Paper: Fourth Industrial Revolution Beacons of Technology and Innovation in Manufacturing, McKinsey and the World Economic Forum, Jan 2019

Don Reisinger, AI Expert Says Automation Could Replace 40% of Jobs in 15 Years, *Fortune*, Jan 10, 2019

Kai-Fu Lee, 10 Jobs That Are Safe in an AI World, *Medium*, Oct 1, 2018

James Manyika, Michael Chui, Mehdi Miremadi, Jacques Bughin, Katy George, Paul Willmott, and Martin Dewhurst, Harnessing Automation for a Future That Works, *McKinsey Global Institute*, Jan 2017

Michael Chui, James Manyika and Mehdi Miremadi, The Countries Most (and Least) Likely to be Affected by Automation, *Harvard Business Review*, Apr 12, 2017

Olivia Solon, Alibaba Founder Jack Ma: AI Will Cause People 'More Pain Than Happiness', *Guardian*, Apr 24, 2017

Jason Hiner, When 85% of the Jobs of 2030 Haven't Been Created Yet, How Do You Prepare?, *Tech Republic*, May 23, 2018

Tim Dutton, An Overview of National Strategies, *Medium*, June 28, 2018

Tim Simonite, Trump's Plan to Keep America First in AI, *Wired*, Feb 11, 2019

New Strategy Outlines Path Forward for AI, US Department of Defense, Feb 2019

Hiawatha Bray, Justin Trudeau Boasts AI in Talk at MIT, *Boston Globe*, May 18, 2018

Lukas Schlogl and Andy Sumner, The Rise of the Robot Reserve Army: Automation and the Future of Economic Development, Work, and Wages in Developing Countries, *Center for Global Development*, Working Paper 487, July 2, 2018

Arjun Kharpal, Davos Founder: World 'Identity Crisis' Driven By Globalization Has Led to Trump's Election, Brexit, *CNBC*, Feb 12, 2017

Guy Standing, *The Precariat: A New Dangerous Class*, Bloomsbury, 2016

Guy Standing, Meet the Precariat, the New Global Class Fueling the Rise of Populism, *World Economic Forum*, Nov 9, 2016

Sam Meredith, Carolin Roth, Fourth Industrial Revolution Expected to Boost Job Creation: CEOs, *CNBC*, Jan 18, 2017

Arjun Kharpal, AI Will Create More Jobs That Can't Be Filled, Not Mass Unemployment, Alphabet's Eric Schmidt Says, *CNBC*, June 16, 2017

Creating the Economy of the Future: How Cutting-Edge Economies Are Transforming Our World, Creating New Jobs – And Protecting Our Data Along the Way, *Wired*, Mar 2018

Chris Weller, Bill Gates Says It's Too Early for Basic Income, But Over Time "Countries Will Be Rich Enough", *Business Insider*, Feb 27, 2017

Fast Company, The One Clear Result of Finland's Basic Income Trial: It Made People Happier, *Medium*, Feb 20, 2019

Catherine Clifford, Billionaire Richard Branson: Extreme Wealth Generated By AI Industry Should Be Used For Cash Handouts, *CNBC*, Oct 10, 2010

Dom Galeon, Universal Basic Income Could Become a Reality, Thanks to This Technology: We Could Make This Happen, *Futurism*, Mar 10, 2017

Marc Howard, How to Start Universal Basic Income with Cryptocurrency, *Medium*, Aug 16, 2018

Basic Income Cryptocurrency Grantcoin, Upgrades and Name Change, *Basic Income Earth Network*, Aug 4 2017

will. i. am, We Need to Own Our Data as a Human Right – and Be Compensated For It, *Economist*, Jan 21, 2019

Jolene Creighton, Experts May Have a Viable Alternative to Universal Basic Income: A radical new idea could be the answer to automation, *Futurism*, Nov 8, 2017

John Thornhill of *Financial Times*, Why Facebook Should Pay US a Basic Income, *Medium*, Aug 8, 2017

Maha Hosain Aziz, *The Global Kid: A Political Comic Book*, 2016

Ivana Kottasova, Egyptian Billionaire Offers to Buy Island for Refugee, *CNN*, Sept 10, 2015
Siobhán O'Grady, Malaysia Has $250 Billion of Debt. The Government is Trying to Crowdfund It, *Washington Post*, June 2, 2018
Malaysian Starts Crowdfunding to Help Reduce Country's Debt, *Strait Times*, May 26, 2018
Disha Daswaney, This Brilliant App Is Launching in the UK to Help Support People with Anxiety, *Evening Standard*, Oct 24, 2017
Sohni Mitter, Thinkladder Wants to Be the Pocket Therapist for Patients of Depression and Anxiety, *Your Story*, Sept 28, 2018
Sarah O'Connor of *Financial Times*, The Robot-Proof Skills That Give Women an Edge in the Age of AI: Men are in danger of being left behind as future well-paid jobs may involve emotional intelligence, *Medium*, Feb 12, 2019
Jonathan Woetzel, Anu Madgavkar, Kweilin Ellingrud, Eric Labaye, Sandrine Devillard, Eric Kutcher, James Manyika, Richard Dobbs, and Mekala Krishnan, How Advancing Women's Equality Can Add $12 Trillion to Global Growth, *Mckinsey Global Institute Report*, Sept 2015

CHAPTER 5: SOCIAL CRISIS

Maha Hosain Aziz, What Are Our Global Values in Today's Post-Hegemonic World?, *Huffington Post*, Aug 29, 2017
Arjun Kharpal, Davos Founder: World 'Identity Crisis' Driven By Globalization Has Led to Trump's Election, Brexit, *CNBC*, Feb 12, 2017
Maha Hosain Aziz, Do We Understand the Global Identity Crisis of Today's Post-Hegemonic World?, *Huffington Post*, Sept 13, 2017
Naomi Grimley, Identity 2016: 'Global Citizenship' Rising, Poll Suggests, *BBC*, Apr 28, 2016
Simon Tisdall, Rise of Xenophobia Is Fanning Immigration Flames in EU and US, *Guardian*, June 22, 2018
Carrie Thompson, UN Security General Warns of Rise in Threats to Human Rights, *Jurist*, Feb 26, 2019
European Islamophobia Report, 2015-2017
Ericha Penzien, Xenophobic and Racist Hate Crimes Surge in the European Union, *Human Rights Brief*, Feb 8, 2017
Jon Henley, Bus Seats Mistaken for Burqas By Members of Anti-Immigrant Group, *Guardian*, Aug 2, 2017
Rage Against Change: Intelligence Report, Issue 166, *Southern Poverty Law Center*, Spring 2019
Barry D. Wood, Storm Clouds of Nationalism Gather Over Eastern Europe, *Marketwatch*, Sept 5, 2017

Vocativ, Refugees Fear Rising Anti-Muslim Backlash In Europe, *Huffington Post*, Jan 13, 2017

Steve Cannane, Geert Wilders, Dutch Right-Wing Politician, Pledges to "De-Islamise" the Netherlands Ahead of Election, *ABC Net*, Mar 12, 2017

Katia Lopez Hodoyan, Denmark Approves Plan to Send Unwanted Migrants to "Virus" Island, *Al Jazeera*, Dec 20, 2018

Pessimism Runs Rampant, Deloitte Millennial Survey, 2017

Tracy Wilkinson, Human Rights Fade from US Foreign Policy Agenda Under Trump, *LA Times*, Apr 5, 2017

Jenna Johnson and Abigail Hauslohner, "I Think Islam Hates Us": A Timeline of Trump's Comments About Islam and Muslims, *Washington Post*, May 20, 2017

Josh Rogin, US State Department Considers Dropping 'Democracy' From Its Mission Statement, *Independent*, Aug 1, 2017

James P. Rubin, The Leader of the Free World Meets Donald Trump, *Politico*, Mar 16, 2017

Kathleen Harris, Trudeau Touts Open Canadian Immigration System In Face of Trump Travel Ban, *CBC News*, June 27, 2017

Jon Sharman, Norway Joins Dutch International Abortion Fund to Combat Donald Trump's Aid Ban, *Independent*, Feb 21, 2017

Nosheen Iqbal, Women Around the World March Against Austerity and Violence, *Guardian*, Jan 19, 2019

Chelsea Bailey and Katie Wong, Global Demonstrations Over Trump's Policies Heat Up Amid Anger Over Travel Ban, *NBC News*, Feb 4, 2017

Luisa Beck, "We Don't Have Time Anymore": In face of climate change, young people across Europe are protesting for their future, Feb 15, 2019

Rebecca Wilson, 25,000 People Just Watched America Ferrera Encourage a Culture of Activism, *Cosmopolitan*, May 19, 2017

Angelina Jolie: Equality for Women Key to Peaceful World, *Washington Post*, Mar 29, 2019

The Dalai Lama and Arthur C. Brooks, The Dalai Lama and Arthur Brooks, All of Us Can Break the Cycle of Hatred, *Washington Post*, Mar 11, 2019

Reuters, Facebook: UN Blames Social Media Giant for Spreading Hatred of Rohingya in Myanmar, *ABC Net,* Mar 12, 2018

Krishnadev Calamur, The World Isn't Prepared to Deal With Possible Genocide In Myanmar, *The Atlantic*, Aug 28, 2018

Paul Mozur, A Genocide Incited on Facebook, With Posts From Myanmar's Military, *New York Times*, Oct 15, 2018

Sudha Ramachandran, Sri Lanka's Anti-Muslim Violence, *Diplomat,* Mar 13, 2018

Michael Safi, Sri Lanka Accuses Facebook Over Hate Speech After Deadly Riots, *Guardian*, Mar 14, 2018

Tribune News Service, 'Kill All Muslims, Don't Let Even One Child of the Dogs Escape': In Sri Lanka, Facebook Struggles to Curb Hate Speech, *South China Morning* Post, Apr 1, 2018

India Hit List of Hindu Muslim Couples Taken Off Facebook, *BBC*, Feb 5, 2018

Matthew Ingram, India Tells WhatsApp to Stop the Deadly Rumor Mill, Somehow, *Columbia Journalism Review*, July 5, 2018

Tom Batchelor, Neo-Nazis Benefiting From Dramatic Rise in Racist Websites to Spread Hate and Incite Violence, UN Warns, *Independent*, Nov 1, 2018

Julia Ebner, *The Rage: The Vicious Circle of Islamist and Far-Right Extremism*, IB Tauris, 2017

Sean Illing, Reciprocal Rage: Why Islamist Extremists and the Far Right Need Each Other, *Vox*, Dec 26, 2018

Jane Coaston, The New Zealand Shooter's Manifesto Shows How White Nationalist Rhetoric Spreads, *Vox*, Mar 18, 2019

Billy Perrigo, The New Zealand Attack Exposed How White Supremacy Has Long Flourished Online, *Time*, Mar 20, 2019

Why White Nationalist Terrorism Is a Global Threat, *Economist*, Mar 21, 2019

Sherisse Pham, Facebook, YouTube and Twitter Struggle to Deal with New Zealand Shooting Video, *CNN*, Mar 15, 2019

Charlie Campbell, The New Zealand Attacks Show How White Supremacy Went From a Homegrown Issue to a Global Threat, *Time*, Mar 21, 2019

Web Needs More Love, Says Its Creator, *BBC,* Nov 2, 2018

James Griffiths, The Sprawling Corruption Scandal That Rocked South Korea, *CNN*, Aug 25, 2017

Dom Phillips, Brazil's Right on the Rise As Anger Grows Over Scandal and Corruption, *Guardian*, July 26, 2017

Thousands Turn Out for Anti-Corruption Protest in Slovakia, *DW*, June 6, 2017

Elizabeth Roberts, Russia's Anti-Corruption Protests Explained, *CNN*, June 12, 2017

Thousands March on Parliament in Anti-Government Protest, *BBC*, July 1, 2017

Protests Erupt in Greece for Second Day Ahead of Major Austerity Vote, *CBS News*, May 18, 2017

Riot Police Fill Streets As Egypt Braces for Austerity Protests, *Enca*, Nov 11, 2016

Kaamil Ahmed, Eight Sudanese Protesters Killed As Anger Rises Over High Living Costs, *Middle East Eye*, Dec 20, 2018

Jennifer Williams, The Violent Protests in Iraq Explained, *Vox*, Sept 8, 2018

Freedom on the Net, *Freedom House*, 2018

Thousands Protests Against Internet Restriction, *Reuters*, Mar 10, 2019

Javier Pallero, Civil Society Unites Against Internet Censorship in Venezuela, *Access Now*, June 1, 2017

Hilary Matfess and Jeffrey Smith, Africa's Attack on Internet Freedom, *Newsweek*, July 23, 2018

Muslim Peace March: Hundreds Take to Cologne Streets to Protest Islamist Terrorism, *Independent*, June 18, 2017

Muslims in Europe Rally Against Extremist Violence, *CBS News*, Sept 26, 2014

'Death to Daesh!' Thousands Protest Against ISIS in Western Afghanistan, *RT*, Jan 4, 2017

Luisa Beck, 'We Don't Have Time Anymore': In Face of Climate Change, Young People Across Europe Are Protesting For Their Future, *Washington Post*, Feb 15, 2019

Leslie Hook, The Climate Activist on Becoming the Face of a Global Movement – And Why She Sees Her Asperger's As a Gift, *Financial Times*, Feb 22, 2019

Jessica Glenza, Alan Evans, Hannah Ellis-Petersen and Naaman Zhou, Climate Strikes Held Around the World, *Guardian*, Mar 15, 2019

Eric Walsh, U.N. Chief Guterres Condemns Racism, Xenophobia: Twitter Post, *US News*, Aug 15, 2017

Philip Pullella, Pope Francis Denounces 'Epidemic Of Animosity' Toward Minorities, *Huffington Post*, Nov 19, 2016

Rebecca Morin, Obama on New Zealand Massacre, *Politico*, Mar 15, 2019

Christchurch Shootings: Jacinda Ardern Calls for Global Anti-Racism Fight, *BBC*, Mar 20, 2019

Maha Hosain Aziz, Three Steps to Reduce ISIS Recruitment in Western Countries, *Huffington Post*, May 5, 2015

Maria Temming, Using Virtual Reality to Treat Social Anxiety, Post-Traumatic Stress Disorders, *Genetic Literacy Project*, Nov 8, 2018

Kendall Teare, New Yale Lab Will Use Virtual Reality Games to Reduce Risks in Teens, *Yale News*, Nov 15, 2017

Simon Parkin, How Virtual Reality Is Helping Heal Soldiers With PTSD, *NBC News*, Mar 16, 2017

Kyle Melnick, Al Jazeera Releases VR Documentary 'I Am Rohingya", *VR Scout*, Oct 1, 2017

Christopher Malmo, A New Virtual Reality Tool Brings the Daily Trauma of the Syrian War to Life, *Motherboard*, Aug 23, 2014

Melissa Hogenboom, Can Virtual Reality Be Used to Tackle Racism?, *BBC*, Nov 28, 2013

Racial Bias Can Be Reduced Through Virtual Reality, European Researchers Say, *University Herald*, Nov 28, 2013

Paul Bloom, It's Ridiculous to Use Virtual Reality to Empathize With Refugees, *The Atlantic*, Feb 3, 2017

Roger Huang, How Blockchain Can Help With The Refugee Crisis, *Forbes*, Jan 27, 2019

Didem Tali, Four AI-Powered Technologies Aimed at Helping Refugees, Dell Technologies, Aug 14, 2018

Michael Chui, Rita Chung, Ashley van Heteren, Using AI to Help Achieve Sustainable Development Goals, UNDP, Jan 21, 2019

Christopher Flavelle, AI Startups Promise to Help Disaster Relief and Evacuation, *Bloomberg Businessweek*, Aug 16, 2018

Michael Chui, Martin Harryson, James Manyika, Roger Roberts, Rita Chung, Ashley van Heteren, Pieter Nel, Notes from the AI Frontier Applying AI for Social Good, Discussion Paper, *McKinsey Global Institute*, Dec 2018

CHAPTER 6: REFLECTING ON OUR UNIQUE GLOBAL LEGITIMACY CRISIS

Denis Diderot and Jean Le Rond d'Alembert (editors), *Encyclopédie: Ou Dictionnaire Raisonnée Des Sciences, Des Arts, et Des Métier*, 1772

Maha Hosain Aziz, #1 Has a New, Global and Tech-Driven Enlightenment Begun? *Medium*, June 26, 2018

Gideon Rose, Who Will Run the World? *Foreign Affairs*, Jan/Feb 2019

Ana Swanson, The World Today Looks A Bit Like It Did Before World War I But What Does That Mean?, *World Economic Forum*, 2017

Elizabeth Mitchell, What Happened to America's Public Intellectuals?, *Smithsonian*, July 2017

David Sessions, The Rise of the Thought Leader: How the Superrich Have Funded a New Class of Intellectual, *New Republic*, June 28, 2017

Amanda L. Gordon, The Identity Crisis of the Ultra-Rich: There have never been more billionaires. So what does it mean to be one? *Bloomberg*, Feb 8, 2019

Lionel Laurent, Make No Mistake, Davos, the Fat Cat Backlash Is Coming, *Bloomberg*, Jan 21, 2019

Anand Giridharadas, *Winner Takes All: The Elite Charade of Changing the World*, Alfred A. Knopf, 2018

Gideon Rachman, Soros Hatred Is a Global Sickness, *Financial Times*, Sept 18, 2017

Kevin Liptak, WH: US Staying Out of Climate Accord, *CNN*, Sept 17, 2017

Kate Vinton, Zuckerberg, Benioff and Other Billionnaires Sound Off on Trump's Decision on Paris Climate Accord, *Forbes*, June 2, 2017

Catherine Clifford, Tech Titans Mark Zuckerberg, Tim Cook, Jack Dorsey Oppose Trump's Ban on Transgender Troops, *CNBC*, July 26, 2017

Arjun Kharpal, Billionaire Jack Ma says CEOs could be robots in 30 years, warns of decades of 'pain' from A.I., internet impact, *CNBC*, Apr 24, 2017

Becky Peterson, It's Not Just Zuckerberg – Slack CEO Stewart Butterfield is a Big Fan of Universal Basic Income, *Business Insider*, Aug 4, 2017

Catherine Clifford, Billionaire Richard Branson: Extreme Wealth Generated By AI Industry Should Be Used for Cash Handouts, *CNBC*, Oct 10, 2017

Catherine Clifford, Elon Musk: Free Cash Handouts "Will Be Necessary" If Robots Take Humans' Jobs, *CNBC*, June 18, 2018

Sandi Doughton, New Report Says Gates Foundation Favors Businesses Not Poor, *Seattle Times*, Jan 20, 2016

Kia Kokalitcheva, Y Combinator Wants to Test a Revolutionary Economic Idea, *Fortune*, May 31, 2016

Y Combinator Research, Basic Income Project Proposal, Overview for Comments and Feedback, Sept 2017

Kathleen Pender, Oakland Group Plans to Launch Nation's Biggest Basic-Income Research Project, *San Francisco Chronicle*, Sept 21, 2017

California Democratic Party, 2018 Platform, Feb 15, 2018

Chris Weller, One of the Biggest VCs in Silicon Valley Is Launching An Experiment That Will Give 3,000 People Free Money Until 2022, *Business Insider*, Sept 21, 2017

Kristine Phillips, Michael Bloomberg Pledges His Own Money to Help UN After Trump Pulls Out of Paris Climate Deal, *Washington Post*, June 3, 2017

Michael Bloomberg, Trump Won't Stop Americans Hitting the Paris Climate Targets. Here's How We Do It?, *Guardian*, Aug 11, 2017

Michael Bloomberg, Our Highest Office, My Deepest Obligation: I'm Not Running for President, But I Am Launching a New Campaign: Beyond Carbon, *Bloomberg*, Mar 5, 2019

Hayley Miller, Bill Gates and Billionaire Buddies Invest $1 Billion In Clean Energy Fund to Fight Climate Change, *Huffington Post*, Dec 13, 2016

Daniella Diaz, Trump: We Cannot Aid Puerto Rico "Forever", *CNN*, Oct 12, 2017

Jake Novak, Elon Musk's Offer to Rebuild Puerto Rico's Electricity Grid is Game Changer, *CNBC*, Oct 9, 2017

Mike Brown, Elon Musk Reveals the Staggering Scale of Tesla's Puerto Rico Solar Projects, *Inverse*, June 4, 2018

Fred Lambert, Tesla Powerwalls and Powerpacks keep the lights on at 662 locations in Puerto Rico during island-wide blackout, says Elon Musk, *Electrek*, Apr 18, 2018

Financial Times, Robot-Proof Skills That Give Women an Edge in the Age of AI, *Medium*, Feb 12, 2019

Dr Maha Hosain Aziz and Brynnan Parish, Let's Create a Social Contract Between Tech Companies and Citizens, *Huffington Post*, Nov 21, 2017

Fulvia Montresor, The Seven Technologies Changing Your World, World Economic Forum, Jan 19, 2016

Josh Lowe, How the iPhone Changed Our Lives, *Newsweek*, Sept 12, 2017

David Streitfeld, Tech Giants, Once Seen As Saviors, Are Now Viewed As Threats, *New York Times*, Oct 12, 2017

Klaus Schwab, The Fourth Industrial Revolution: What It Means, How To Respond, *World Economic Forum*, Jan 14, 2016

Elizabeth Dwoskin and Adam Entous, Google Says Russia Tried to Influence US Election Using Adverts on YouTube and Gmail, *Independent*, Oct 9, 2017

Mike Snider, Your Data Was Probably Stolen in Cyberattack in 2018 and You Should Care, *USA Today*, Jan 1, 2019

Tim Worstall, Lloyd's – Extreme Cyberattack Could Cost $120 Billion, As Much As 0.2% Of Global GDP, *Forbes*, July 17, 2017

#MeToo - Sexual Harassment Stories Sweep Social Media After Weinstein Allegations, *Reuters*, Oct 16, 2017

Tom Embury-Dennis, Man Who Invented "Like" Button Deletes Facebook App Over Addiction Fears, *Independent*, Oct 6, 2017

Melissa G. Hunt, Rachel Marx, Courtney Lipson, Jordyn Young, No Moe FOMO: Limiting Social Media Decreases Loneliness and Depression, *Journal of Social & Clinical Psychology*, Vol. 37, No. 10, pg 751-768, Dec 2018

Doug Criss, A Mom Found Videos on YouTube Kids that Gave Children Instructions on Suicide, *CNN*, Feb 25, 2019

What If Large Tech Firms Were Regulated Like Sewage Companies: Being Treated As Utilities Is Big Tech Firm's Biggest Long-Term Threat, *Economist*, Sept 23, 2017

Rob Picheta, Instagram Is Leading Social Media Platform for Child Grooming, *CNN*, Mar 1, 2019

Adam Lashinsky, Data Regulation Is Coming For Big Tech, *Fortune*, Mar 1, 2018

Rachel Coldicutt, The Tech Industry Needs a Moral Compass, *Medium*, Nov 13, 2017

Laurence Dodds, Sir Tim Berners-Lee launches 'Magna Carta for the web' to save internet from abuse, *Telegraph*, Nov 5, 2018